Modern Experim...

Brahmacharya under microscope

-Jatin Shankar

All rights reserved; no part of this publication may be reproduced or transmitted by any means, electronic, mechanical, photocopying or otherwise, without the prior permission of the author.

This Digital edition published by Slateword Publishing House Ltd in 2016

Text Copyright © Prem Kumar 2016

(Writing as Jatin Shankar)

Edited By Jyoti Singh

Cover Design by Nikhil Chopra, Slateword Ltd.

Book Design and production by Suresh Sharma, Slateword Ltd.

The moral right of the author has been asserted.

To,
the spirit of science

INTRODUCTION	**9**
PART1: OVERVIEW OF SOME EXPERIMENTS	**21**
THE CONNECTION BETWEEN REPRODUCTION AND LIFE SPAN	21
Graph1: Qualitative relationship between fecundity and lifespan in C. elegans (Linda Partridge, 2005)	*23*
Graph 2: Lifespan vs. reproductive pattern in Rotifers (Terry W. Snell, 1977)	*24*
ALL ABOUT EUNUCHS	26
The disaster at a mental hospital	*28*
Graph 3: Survival curve for 100 castrated and intact males	*29*
The eunuchs from Korea	*30*
Eunuchs that grew back lost hair!	*30*
Effect of Castration on other organisms	*30*
THE COST OF REPRODUCTION	30
The ejaculates from Japanese macaque	*31*
The Adders during mating season	*33*
THE COST OF REPRODUCTION IN FEMALE	34
THE AGING MAN	35
On brain	*36*
On rest of the body	*37*
WORKS CITED	**38**
PART2: THE GRAND THEORY OF CELIBACY	**41**
DO WE KILL OUR SELF IN THE END, OR THE CIRCUMSTANCES KILL US?	43

- *Programmed theory of aging:* *43*
- *Non-programmed theory of aging:* *44*

THE LIFE HISTORY THEORY AND THE SUICIDAL WORLD 47

THREE IMAGINARY WORLDS 54

- *Graph 4: Population survival pattern in an aging and non-aging population* *56*
- *The cost of dead bodies* *58*

OUR LOGIC TILL NOW 59

- *Graph 5: Relationship between lifespan and fecundity of organism under various resource constraints* *61*

BREAKING THE SILENCE ON BRAHMACHARYA 66

THE SCIENTIFIC THEORY OF BRAHMACHARYA 68

- *Some questions against Brahmacharya:* *70*

A SMALL CLARIFICATION 74

MIXING MILK IN WATER 82

A CANDLE IN THE DARKNESS 86

PART3: PHILOSOPHICAL CONSEQUENCE OF BRAHMACHARYA 89

IF EVERYONE PRACTICES BRAHMACHARYA OR CELIBACY, HOW WILL OUR SPECIE ADVANCE? 89

IS THERE ANYTHING MORE EXCITING THAN SEX? 90

ON HAPPINESS 94

BACK MATTER 99

ABOUT THE AUTHOR 99

Introduction

This Book is about Celibacy, or Brahmacharya, and an account of some modern biological theory and experiments that put it to test. Why? Not to force the reader- you, to stop having sex! Neither is this book meant to make you feel guilty about sex, nor to taboo the concept. Then why is this book? ...why put up this awkward topic?

To scientifically analyze the truth or possibly the falsehood behind the philosophy of celibacy, and the claims that it makes. This book exists to seek the truth, whatever be it, using strong scientific premise laid down by solid modern quantitative laboratory experiments and theoretical arguments. This book intends to speak the truth.

I think that it is wrong to blindly follow celibacy just because one believes in its benefits without putting one's belief to test, scientifically. Maybe blindly believing in something would have been okay 500 years ago, when biological science was not as developed as it is now. At that time, people had to go by their gut, believing things out of experience and intuition, without conducting experiments to test their beliefs. Because there were few means to test hypothesis at that time... Science was less developed then. Advanced technology was absent. 500 years ago, had not people gone by their gut, they would end up living a meaningless life- a life without *any* philosophy or beliefs.

Now fast forward 500 years... Is it possible that on one hand, we have religious books claiming amazing benefits about Celibacy, and on the other hand, we have an ever advancing biological science probing the fundamental questions about life and nature of consciousness; and yet these two not having an opinion about each other? This is not possible. Biological science does hold an opinion about the theory of Celibacy. This book is intended to bring the opinion forward.

We have a never ending debate about benefits and uselessness of Celibacy. Some think that it is downright superstition based upon a line of thinking proposed by the primitive man, and others, the (*blind*) believers claim miracles associated with the practice of Celibacy.

So, the question is, can we end this debate? Can we settle it? Does the modern biological knowledge of present time support the philosophy behind Celibacy? If yes, then will it support *all* the claims made by it, or only a few selected ones? How true is the concept of Brahmacharya? Does the intuition of the primitive man hold some underlying reason behind it? Or is the concept of Brahmacharya simply a way through which sex was tabooed in primitive, uneducated societies? Is Celibacy the method through which defeatist and pessimist people punished themselves by controlling their sexual impulse at all cost, without any reason, just for the sake of doing it...?

Why should sex be abolished? Why should someone practice celibacy for a few claimed health benefits of it, when the same can obviously be achieved through a good diet? Why should people give up the pleasures of mating that have been programmed in their genes through evolution? Why should this topic be even discussed?

Well, that was too much attack on a silly belief in one day...! But what if the skeptics of Brahmacharya do not realize the entire truth? What if the beaten up philosophers supporting Brahmacharya are actually supporting truth masked behind mysticism and inability to explain its own self? What if there exist *tons of modern biological data in the form of experiments and theories* supporting the concept of Brahmacharya, revealing the true nature of life... What if sexual excitement is nothing but a method used by few funny mortals, dancing around on a funny planet, not knowing anything about *how* they came to be and *where* they are going, and having no clue whatsoever about the truth of the cosmos? Dropped into existence by a funny system of laws they do not understand, what if they are living on a small volatile blue spherical speck floating in a dark cosmos filled with other specks- the stars and dust, and what if the speck that they call earth is enjoying a temporary period of peace, sandwiched by eras of cosmic chaos caused by supernovae explosions, meteorite showers and what not… What if we are mere centuries away from the next catastrophic invasion from heavens…?

What if we live in a world about which we understand nothing, and what if our sexual stimulation is a small insignificant scheme at play to ensure that we keep our numbers up, and wait for few geniuses like Ramanujan and Newton, who rise above their mortal sexual self in order to contribute to the future of our world in ways more than that promised by sex…? What if the next genius is *you* but you are still stuck around mere sexual aspect of life, completely missing the greater abstract beauty that Van Gogh noticed in the world, and which Picasso tried to capture… What if there flows an ocean of abstract truth through us, and even slight interaction with that ocean can give you a life changing experience? What if our little speck is reverse counting its remaining time, and we have to understand the abstract part of the cosmos, of physical reality, so that we can avert the heavenly catastrophe or evacuate this planet, before it is too late? What if the biggest task that we have is to outlive our own speck, our own blue planet nearing a disaster, somehow?

Mere reproductive success is not the truth about life. Had it been, Van Gogh would not paint *Starry night*… Ramanujan would not dream about equations that describe the thoughts of god… Don't you see? We have risen above the material way of things... we have started exploring the abstract domain of the universe. Our curiosity has nothing to do with our sexuality, and both have a separate reason for existing. Both are completely mutually exclusive, and both have been infused by evolution into us. But sexuality had been there for sometime... it used to be the first priority once. But recently, the priorities have changed... Humanity has started dreaming the lustful dreams of science... Maybe science is a higher level of sexuality... Maybe nature knows that earth will not remain for long... maybe nature has already witnessed a premature planet die... maybe nature wants us to live... maybe this is why we dream... maybe this is why we stare at the night sky, the stars... maybe this is the reason for the existence of mathematics... maybe curiosity has a very supreme reason to be...

....

In Hindu religion, there exists *Hanuman*, the monkey god, who was a celibate. There also exist many Asian monks and yogis who are celibate. Among them was Swami Vivekananda, the famous monk from the 19th century, who was also a nationalist. He established *Ramakrishna* mission, an institute for monks and scholars. Today this institute publishes many books at highly subsidized prices from Vivekananda and other monks on various subjects aimed for the personal development of youth and general readers, based upon the teachings of *Vedas and Puranas* (ancient manuscripts). It is through these books that I first came across the concept of Brahmacharya. As a young child, the philosophy of Brahmacharya impressed me. The book talked about energy, and how when directed away from sexual thoughts, it could directly nourish the brain in unimaginable ways. I passionately began pursuing Brahmacharya. But soon, clouds of doubt started hovering over the clear sky of my mind. In the spirit of science, I became skeptical.

How could I be sure that the claims made in the books were correct? They had no scientific experiments to back them up!

Brahmacharya, according to the philosophers, is complete abstinence from all sexual impulses in life- from one's thought, speech and act. This state of mind and body is considered the most suitable for learning. Brahmacharya is the thing of students. Its benefits, according to the scriptures, are appalling, and I will list a few:

- Increased body immunity
- Increased cognitive ability; few scripts claim that 12 years of strict celibacy results in amazing regeneration of new nerve circuits in the brain that facilitates learning 'new' things. Hence philosophers claim that Brahmacharya gives the brain high amount of plasticity.
- No degradation over age. A celibate does not ages.
- There are some obvious psychological effects arising from previous points, like fearlessness, tirelessness, creativity, increased concentration etc.

One can see that Brahmacharya, as claimed, has the potential of transforming the quality of life of a person. It should be noted that the *Vedas, Puranas* and philosophers provide *no* biological experiment as proof of these claims. Their *science* was mere theoretical, arising from thought, experience and intuition, and I credit them for this and *this* only. I will praise them for coming over a partially correct theory, but I will point out that they did not understand its mechanism correctly.

One particularly impressive example of the correctness of their intuition is their mechanism of tradeoff of energy in the body. The philosophers believed that sexual energy can be diverted towards spiritual and intellectual pursuit, and can directly fuel the brain and body. It is surprising that such a tradeoff of energy between different life processes like 'reproduction', 'repair and maintenance of the body', growth, neurogenesis and immunity indeed exists in our present biological theories! The biologists have noted that in rats, there exists inverse relation between the amount of fecundity and lifespan, and increasing one result in the decrease of the other! We will discuss this and some more similar experiments in detail soon.

The idea behind this book is that the claims made by the ancient philosophers are very clearly stated, hence making their theory a scientifically testable one. Medical science and biology today has made immense progress. If there are so many benefits of Brahmacharya, then I am sure that evidence for it can be easily found at various regions in the sea of our scholarly articles. I found the evidence! I found many evidences… Yet I found no official statement from the biologists in attempt to develop a complete scientific theory about Brahmacharya. Why is everyone silent about it? …Maybe because our scientists do not want to break the ignorance and the bliss of the common people. Maybe the world is so much sex-driven that any talk of celibacy sounds immature and superstitious. Well, I have discovered that everyone is superstitious if one will give oneself few hours of introspection. So, why not take some time out of the busy life and study this book with me and try to find out the nature of the ultimate truth about life?

Now, the ancient philosophers, as intuitive as they were, faced pitfalls of not doing lab experiments only shortly. After explaining the theory of tradeoff of energy within the body, they went on to claim that the sexual energy, when channelized, converts into *Ojas*, the highest form of energy available in the body, stored in the brain. It is claimed that all types of energy that exists in the body, if channelized, can be converted into

Ojas. For example, it is claimed that even muscular energy, if disused, transforms to become *Ojas*.

When body digests food, the best part of the food too goes on to become *Ojas*, they claim. And *Ojas* is nothing but the indicator of charisma that a person possesses. The more *Ojas* you have, the keener, sharper and stronger you are. Now, it must be noted that the source of *Ojas* is food, so you do not need to be celibate to possess it. But the thing is, when sexual energy is diverted, even for a moment, for some higher cause, like scientific, artistic or social breakthrough, then it transforms into *Ojas*. The philosophers claim that god is nothing but something all the energy possessed by whom is in the form of *Ojas*, and that if a human does that, he becomes god.

Well, these topics deserve the mysticism used while telling them. But when I once asked a Biology professor of mine whether there exists some region in the brain acting as a storehouse of energy, I got a disappointing answer. I was actually asking about the physical location of *Ojas,* since the philosophers claimed it existed in the brain. My Biology professor replied that there exists no such specialized structure in the brain whatsoever, as far as modern biology understands it.

So, does *Ojas* exist? It turns out that the ancient Hindu philosophers were not being literal when they described the location of *Ojas* to be the brain. So, this means that they had no formulae to know the truth about the world without conducting experiments. Hence, we must take whatever we are told, with few grains of salt. So, it is all the more necessary to study the science behind Brahmacharya, and to clear this unnecessary fog around the topic with the help of science, so that the skeptic and the atheist also enter the domain which earlier permitted only the believers and the theists.

But Before continuing with the book, I would like to point out what this book is *not* about:

1. This book does not focus on the spiritual aspect of practicing Brahmacharya. I will not be giving you the spiritual reasons to practice celibacy, although you are free to discover some reasons for yourself! This book is open for atheist and theists alike, and broadly anyone who would like to study some scientific experiments before believing anything. So, theist, atheist, the maverick, the heretic, the critic, the skeptic and all the other people who 'tic' are invited to study this book and share their own opinion about what they think directly to the author through author email or at the website; as indicated in the back matter of this book.
2. This book completely rejects Taoist sexual practice of semen *injaculation* (or retrograde ejaculation) - the process through which a man does *not* ejaculates semen during orgasm. This is achieved by using physical methods like blocking the passage of semen by applying pressure on a certain nerve, or alternatively not crossing the 'point-of-no-return' during orgasm. Although I appreciate their apprehension over the health concerns associated with the loss of semen since it will be soon seen in the book that several experiments do suggest that ejaculation is quite costly for the organism, yet the retention of these nutrients cannot explain the amazing benefits that is claimed by the philosophy of Celibacy. For example, a simple dietary change can supplement the entire nutrients lost during ejaculation, hence destroying the belief of Taoists that reabsorbing semen can have special benefit beyond nutrition. Why bother injaculating when few nutrition supplements can restore all the nutrients lost in ejaculation?

It is interesting to observe that where the Taoist theory gets destroyed due to logic, the concept of Brahmacharya survives. How this is possible I will discuss shortly in the book, but currently I leave the readers with a puzzle: In an experiment done on rats, an inverse relationship between their rate of reproduction and their longevity has been found. It was done by giving the rats less than normal yet nutritive diet, so that they remain hungry but do not starve. What do you think happened? The rats stopped reproducing. The reason is simple. During a food-scarcity situation, having offspring would be a bad idea and waste of energy. But, surprisingly, in such a dietary restricted scenario, their lifespan always increases!

This means that if we decrease the supply of food, the rate of aging actually *decreases*! Moreover, if you provide a group of rats with surplus amount of food, their lifespan remains constant, while rate of reproduction in them (or fecundity) increases exponentially. So, for some mysterious reason that we would soon discuss in this book, there is no benefit of 'extra' nutrients in the body, provided you are already taking a balanced diet!

This means that the Taoist philosophers have it all wrong when they insist on conserving semen. The real science here, like all science, is complicated.

We will soon see that extra nutrition can have only minimal effect on the rate of aging. It is the body priorities that have to be changed… To understand the true cost of reproduction, we will have to study the delicate biological mechanism of life. We will soon note that an organism investing energy over sex is not doing a fancy activity. Too much is at stake. The amount of energy that organisms invest on reproduction decides who lives till eternity in the form of their own offspring. Sex is special. It is the ticket to immortality for life, since without sex, no specie can survive. At the same time, it is the ticket to old age. Do not judge as yet. I will explain everything shortly. I have a very good reason for what I say, which is why this book exists. But over that, I have experimental results supporting this theory, so our palace of thoughts has its root on solid unshakable ground.

3. This book does not ask you to practice celibacy. Just have a scientific look towards it. This book combines biology with philosophy, and mind my words, some understanding of biology can give a philosophical meaning to life. Other than that, this book can give back meaning of life to those who think they have lost it to porn or sex addiction. This book might make them understand that biologically, there exists more to life than sexual ecstasy.

Now, in this book, we are not going to study the metabolism of life to prove our theories. Instead, we are going to study some physical properties of life to come to conclusions that the same metabolic processes must exist in order to satisfy the experimental data. In this way, our theory is similar to the theory of thermodynamics studied in physics. Thermodynamics studies any given situation using some macroscopic physical properties like pressure and temperature of air to describe the results of an experiment which more accurately depends upon many microscopic entities like the size and the structure of air molecules, and their positions and velocities at any given moment of time. Hence, we are going to have a bird eye view of biology instead of getting lost in the intricate details.

Now, I will like to describe the structure of this book.

To maintain the scientific spirit of this book, I first provide the undeniable scientific facts arising directly from experiments. I will describe the results of each experiment, and also provide you with the sources so that you yourself may check the actual research paper to study the details. Please note that some of the research papers are behind a pay wall, and you would need a university affiliation to read them, or you will personally have to visit the library of a nearby university for the same. You can also contact a friend who has access, or directly contact the authors. But this will really be worth it, believe me.

In the second part of the book, we will be discussing the biological theories to explain the experimental data. The biological theories provided in this book can be challenged, of course, so I advise you to have a critical outlook throughout this book. If you think that you have found a loophole in this theory, or a better theory, then you can give your feedback at the website indicated at the back of this book so that we can discuss the matter further!

Finally, after establishing a scientific niche for Brahmacharya, we will rise a little higher than that to discuss some philosophical implications and paradoxes arising from our latest development of the matter, along with their possible resolution.

Part1: Overview of some Experiments

In this part, we will be discussing several experiments that support the idea of Brahmacharya or Celibacy. Although we will be discussing them in all the details, I provide you the sources to the full text articles. Also, it should be noted that there exist a whole network of interconnected research and experiments in this area, as well as many open questions and many aspect of the experiments yet to be inspected. So, just like any other field of science, this is an ever-growing area of research, and I will update you with the recent progress on the websites indicated in the back matter of this book.

The connection between reproduction and life span

For at least 50 years, it has been known in biological circles that there exists an inverse relation between the fecundity (the rate of reproduction) and lifespan of an organism. Increase in rate of reproduction directly decreases lifespan of an organism, and vice versa. This result has been established in many experiments done on organisms like mice, drosophila, chaetognatha, beetles, lizards, rotifers and some plants.

The method used in laboratory to reduce (or control) fecundity in these organisms is called *dietary restriction*. Dietary restriction refers to a situation in which food supplies required by an organism to lead a normal life is cut short. Dietary restriction is an important tool used in laboratory to study how an organism would behave during many naturally occurring food-scarcity situations, like famine, flood, climatic changes etc. During a dietary restriction experiment, the organism tries to survive through the food-scarcity scenario hoping for the things to get better in the coming future. Drawing an analogy, when the battery of my phone is down and there is no electricity, I try to avoid using it unnecessarily, bring down the brightness of the screen to save battery and mostly wait through the *disaster* for the electricity to come back... What will *you* do if you are put on a restricted diet? Let's try to find out by studying what a rat would do in such a situation instead-

One of the most remarkable traits observed in an animal subjected to dietary restriction is reduced fecundity or rate of reproduction. This makes sense, because if there is no food to eat, the last thing you would want is having a child-birth. What will the child eat? Hence, all the animals subjected to dietary restriction show drastic decrease in sexual inclination. This indeed supports the fact that in some religion, people fast on a religious day before the time for worshiping... this might simply be to reduce the sexual inclination for the day! One must credit the ancient philosophers sometimes for their keen observational skills!

The other important result of dietary restriction observed on organisms will *shock* you. *They live longer!* (Stearns, 1976) (Weindruch, 1996) Yes, their lifespan *increases* when *less* food is given to them! Unbelievable, is it not?

Of course if you reduce the food supplies to make them really tiny then the animal would die out of starvation. But that is not the point. The point is that organisms do not live longest when they are well fed. They start living longer when the food supplies start *dwindling*!

These results have been well established through many decades of experiments. The trouble is- how does one explain them?

Here I will like to make a correction to what I have just said few paragraphs back. When we said that the organism stops reproducing, we implied that the fecundity is reduced because it becomes a *useless* activity, because the kids will most likely not survive a food-scarcity situation. But wait, to explain the fact that their lifespan *increases* during dietary restriction, our previous argument is not enough. We must conclude that the very *act* of not reproducing had some mysterious benefit! The act of not reproducing has a latent ability to increase the lifespan, and so much of it that it even outdoes the negative effect of a reduced diet! Is reproduction shortening our life? If yes, then *why*?

Graph1: Qualitative relationship between fecundity and lifespan in C. elegans (Linda Partridge, 2005)

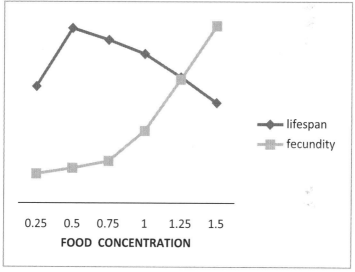

Does this experiment nod in the approval towards the philosophy of Brahmacharya?

We will study the theory trying to explain this experiment shortly in the second part of this book. I hate to leave an experiment unexplained, but the idea is to present all experimental data we have at one place, so that when we discuss the theory, we have sharp idea as to why we are reading this book *at all*. ...*B*ecause there exist some paradoxical experiments, and because we are curious humans who settle at nothing but the truth... the complete, unabridged one.

I will now tell you one more interesting finding from these experiments through graph 2. This graph relates the lifespan and the number of offspring in rotifers, a kind of microscopic animal. One will notice that this graph, obtained from experiment, confirms, from another perspective, the belief that an inverse relation between the lifespan and fecundity exists in organisms.

Graph 2: Lifespan vs. reproductive pattern in *Rotifers* (Terry W. Snell, 1977)

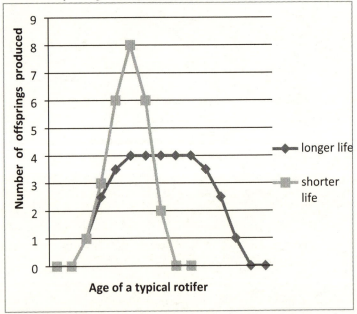

In this experiment, it was found that the rotifers which gave birth to more number of offspring at a time had a marked shorter life than those who gave birth to less number of offspring.

So, I will leave you with these facts, and a pestering question- Why should sexual reproduction be harming us? If the loss is nutritive in nature, why does not overfeeding *decreases* the lifespan of an organism and a little underfeeding *increases it?* Why cannot the nutritional cost that is brought upon an organism through reproduction be regained through a better diet? Can there be a reasonable scientific explanation which can explain this paradox?

I will like to point out one last thing. Many people may wonder as to how one can draw inferences about things that affect a human body from experiments that were done on animals like mice, lizards and drosophila? Well, there are several reasons why we can safely make these inferences:

1. Life on earth enjoys a common ancestry, as a result of which, an unrelated animal like a mouse has more in common with you than you may imagine. For example, a cell taken from the body of a mouse is practically indistinguishable from a cell from our own body, given that we are not too much critical about the details. In fact, mouse is considered almost human by experimental biologists, this often making them the ideal lab rats in many of the biological experiments.
2. The traits that we are analyzing in these animals are very fundamental ones. For example, we are studying the response of these animals during a dietary restricted scenario. Such a response should not get affected by any evolutionary difference that may exist between, let us say, a human being and a mouse, because the survival strategy that *should* be used by both of them is reasonably the same- to conserve

energy during the situation. In other words, the experiment we discussed is not a very complicated or specie specific one. We are *not* trying to understand the response of the human body to a certain hormone by studying the response of the body of a mouse to the same. This would be too complicated, although given the similarities between a human and a mouse; even such experiments are often carried out by the clever biologists. So, the experiment that we *are* studying in this book is too general, and a parallel between the results obtained from the experiments that are done on animals and those that should be there if similar experiments are done on human being, should be easy to establish.

3. All organisms reproduce, some sexually, other asexually, but the idea is just the same.

Hence, we can safely conclude that after studying the experiments done on any organism we can always draw some reasonable conclusions, which apply on our own self.

All about Eunuchs

In the previous experiment, we saw how temporary reduction in fecundity, caused by dietary restriction, caused a healthy increase in the lifespan of the organisms, indicating a slowdown in the rate of their aging. So a natural question that arises is- What will happen if fecundity is lowered using methods other than the gentle dietary restriction?

Can castration increase the lifespan of an organism?

After all, castration is but a way to lower the fecundity. So, there should be an increase in the lifespan of the organism following castration. And there is, as we will see shortly.

But before that, I would like to put a disclaimer. Castration, for the sake of celibacy, is not suggested in this book, so the readers are advised not to get any bright ideas in this direction.

Other than many obvious reasons for this, there may be many biological disadvantages of castration. For example, it should not be assumed that human sexual organs only play the sole purpose of reproduction.

Other than that, it should be noted that Brahmacharya is not equivalent to castration. While the former is a state of the body in which the biological priorities are naturally changed for a higher scientific, spiritual or social purpose, the latter is more like a shock over the body, and simply an inability to reproduce.

Hence, while being aware of the obvious differences between a celibate and a eunuch (a male that has been castrated for medical reasons or otherwise), we now focus on the similarities for the sake of scientific argument. We will draw analogous conclusions on the effect of celibacy on an organism by studying effects of castration on eunuchs, while being aware that they are not exactly the same, yet have a striking similarity, namely, decreased fecundity, caused by philosophical or scientific reasons in the former, and simple biological inability in the latter. So here we go-

Human beings have been castrated, and are castrated even today, for several reasons. Historically, it was used as means of torture or punishment over criminals and war prisoners. Castrated men were also considered religiously pure in many societies and were allotted as soldiers, usually posted as the defenders of the harem. In Christian churches, young boys who sang in church were castrated before puberty so that they retain their high pitch voice throughout life. Today, castrations are done for medical reasons, and usually chemical castration through drugs is preferred over the actual mutilation of testes. Other than that, some people also go through castration to attain a feminine look, like *Hijras* in south Asian countries.

Now, experimental evidence suggests that castration delays aging in several organisms! Equipped with the experimental fact that lifespan and fecundity are inversely related, it naturally follows that this should be so.

The disaster at a mental hospital

In 20th century, forced castration on some of trouble creating patients in a thus infamous mental hospital was carried out. The act of castration was done to induce a calmer personality over the patients, and shocking as it may be, and even criminal, this disaster was scientifically documented to study the effect of castration on longevity of an organism.

The researchers discovered that castration increased the lifespan (James B. Hamilton, 1969) of the patients! Moreover, the experiment also established that younger the patients were at the time of castration, the longer was their life expectancy!

I will like to point few strong points about this specific experiment and how it was conducted:-

1. Both the castrated as well as intact patients studied in this experiment lived in the same condition, hence removing the problems of different life styles and the effects that it may have on lifespan.
2. All the patients that were castrated were completely identical to rest of the population on every basis other than behavioral which was what had stimulated the castration. This means that on the basis of health, there was no difference in the choice of patients that were castrated, implying that the two groups were completely identical and the results brought forward from this experiments can give out reasonable conclusions. This is a remarkable feature of this experiment because today castration is carried out due to medical reasons, and hence a similar study done today will fail to bring reasonable conclusions

because such patients cannot be compared with healthy individuals.
3. This experiment considers a total of 297 castrated male cases, against 735 intact normal patients. Hence, the numbers are large and we can expect the irregularities to cancel each other out…

Here is a qualitative graphical representation of the findings of this experiment to give you a better idea of the statistics-

Graph 3: Survival curve for 100 castrated and intact males

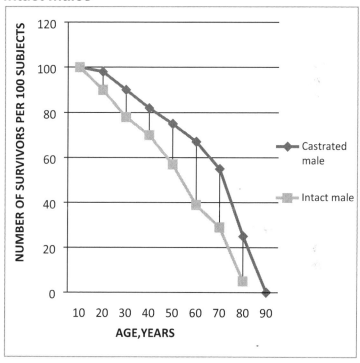

Notice how half of the castrated male population in the experiment survived till the age of 70 whereas the intact population got halved at about 55 years of age!

The eunuchs from Korea
In this recent study, lifespan of 81 Eunuchs that existed in Korea between 16th and 19th century were studied based on documents that were retrieved. A shocking revelation was that the eunuchs were found to live 14 years extra (Min, 2012) than the average lifespan of the normal people at that time! In fact, 3 out of the 81 eunuchs that were studied had lived more than 100 years, suggesting that in fact eunuchs experience a much slower aging.

Eunuchs that grew back lost hair!
There exist other interesting physiological features associated with eunuchs. Like, it has been observed that a man castrated before the appearance of male pattern baldness does not get bald. In fact, people who were castrated after getting aging related balding have been noted to grow back lost hair! (HAMILTON, 1960)

These facts hint towards anti aging effects of castration, which seems to confirm the experiments we have studied previously.

Effect of Castration on other organisms
The effects of castration on other organisms like dog, bull, mice and salmon fish has been well studied in biology, and include marked increase in lifespan (Robertson, 1961)

Hence, the fact that traits like sexual reproduction, body repair and maintenance comes with cost associated with it is established.

The cost of Reproduction
Everyone agrees that reproduction is costly for a female. For a female, the costs involve gamete formation, giving birth to offspring and lactation (in mammals).

For a male the costs are quite different and involve the manufacture of semen, mate searching, courtship, copulation and male-male combat. Traditionally, inferring from the small size of ejaculate, which is about 3ml to 5ml in healthy human being, it was believed that the cost of spermatogenesis in male is very small compared with other costs involved, hence justifying the famous term that *sperm is cheap*. But is it really so? The following experiments condemn the idea-

The ejaculates from Japanese macaque

This experiment was done on male Japanese macaques, a kind of primate monkey. These primates, if not allowed to reproduce, would masturbate to ejaculate, and are known to do this at least once a day during mating season, through sex or otherwise, and as much as 6 times daily if we are to observe the dominant alpha male mating with several females.

Now, this experiment collected 21 samples of semen freshly ejaculated after masturbation, and calculated that each medium sized ejaculate had a calorific value of 8.1 kJ. You must note that 8 kJ is costly for Japanese macaques because their body weight is about 10 kg.

Next the experimentalists calculated the BMR of the animals. What is BMR? Well, BMR or Basal metabolic rate is the energy expended by an organism while at complete rest, when even the digestive system is inactive, meaning that it can be calculated only at least after 12 hours of fasting.

The scientists found that an average macaque spends about 1% of its daily BMR value through every ejaculation, implying that for a male ejaculating 6 times a day in the mating season, the energy investment is 6%! (Ruth Thomsen, 2006) This means that a sexually active Japanese macaque spends about 1 to 6 percent of the energy required to keep itself alive for a day in the form of seminal loss. Drawing a parallel between a macaque and a human being is difficult, although both are primates, yet we get a general idea that ejaculation does bear a cost for the male.

It is worth noting that this research only includes the calorific value of semen, and not the energy required for the production of sperm cells and seminal fluids. Spermatogenesis is known to take about 3 months in human beings!

Suppose you have made a painting on paper, which your friend suggests you burn so that both of you can enjoy the heat from the flame during a cold winter night. Since the painting is your hard work, you will refuse to this, yet your friend fails to attribute it any significance thinking it's burning as a loss of just few kilojoules of heat and nothing more!

Same is true with this research on Japanese macaques. It quantifies the energy content in semen, finding it significant. Yet, this is not the whole truth, because the *production* of semen has costs associated with it too, which has not been analyzed in this experiment. Semen is not equivalent to the energy content of its constituent particles in the same way as a Smartphone is not equivalent to the energy content of the constituent metal and nonmetal going in its manufacture. A Smartphone is something more than the energy obtained by burning it!

Spermatogenesis is special as it contains the genetic material which will decide the structure of the future generation, hence explaining why it takes 3 months to manufacture a sperm cell. Spermatogenesis takes stem cell time and also have metabolic costs associated because the sperm cells have to be checked and rechecked for genetic defects.

Hence, we must be clear that all that this paper measures is the calorific investment of the macaques in the form of ejaculation with respect to their daily BMR value. Interestingly, the next experiment that we are going to discuss quantifies the energy investment in production of sperm cells and seminal fluids only.

The Adders during mating season

An interesting fact that several experiments on seasonally breeding male primates have revealed is that they 'reduce their testes size during the non-breeding season, implying that testicular tissue, spermatogenesis and ejaculates are costly for the primates and hence worth saving'! (Harcourt, 1995) But to get a more quantitative idea about the cost of spermatogenesis, our next clue comes from the reptilian world.

An experiment done on Adders, a small, poisonous snake found in Asia and Europe, confirms that the male Adders suffer *significant* loss of body weight during their two months long mating season, hence confirming the cost of reproduction theory. But the experimentalists initially made the fatal error of assuming that this loss in weight was mainly being caused by the mate-searching, copulation, courtship and male-male combat that happened within the Adder community, with the effect due to spermatogenesis not contributing significantly.

But they decided to correct their mistake and repeat the experiment when they were prompted by *another* research theorizing 'a significant cost due to spermatogenesis in organisms'. They quickly realized that if spermatogenesis was costly in organisms then male Adders were the ideal candidates to confirm this.

The reason is this: the cost of spermatogenesis in males is *very* difficult to determine for obvious reasons that you cannot pinpoint whether the cost is coming from spermatogenesis or something else. So, one cannot tell whether it is spermatogenesis which is consuming the energy or the other sexual behaviors like mate searching and male-male combats. But adders are very interesting animals in this respect! They do not do *anything* at all but take rest when spermatogenesis is going on in them!

Their mating season can be divided into two parts:

1. The first part involves the phase of spermatogenesis, when the adders simply bask in the sun, do not feed and do not involve in any physical activity. This phase lasts for about one month.
2. The second phase comes when the adders become active and mate-searching, copulation, courtship and male-male combats begin. This phase lasts for about 3 weeks. The males again do not feed in this phase either, meaning that they do not feed throughout their mating season.

What the experimentalists did was to measure the weight of the adders individually before, during and after each phase, in order to discover the rate of weight loss whole through the season. The weight loss should directly correlate with the energy expended in reproduction because the adders do not feed through the season, and are very unlikely to defecate or urinate since they go into hibernation with empty bowels.

The experimentalists were hence surprised to find that the weight loss during the spermatogenesis phase was equal (Mats Olsson, 1997) to that lost in the second phase which involved actual physical exertion. Earlier, they had assumed that the second phase was the sole contributor to the loss of weight in the Adders! Hence, this experiment directly shows that there exists a significant metabolic cost due to spermatogenesis in an organism!

The cost of reproduction in female

One does not need to refer to research papers to convince oneself that reproduction is costly for a female. It is a common knowledge that females need special diet during pregnancy and lactation, implying that there exists a cost associated. The reason why the female cost of reproduction is well understood is because a major part of it is concentrated at specific periods of time, let us say, pregnancy and lactation. Also, a female tends to lose reproductive capabilities after middle age. Their reproductive pattern hence involves exhausting the body during short durations of strains and then giving it up altogether after a while. Contrasting this with male, a male human being practically retain his reproductive capabilities till death, implying that the costs are more uniformly distributed throughout life, and hence less dramatic at any given moment of time.

To understand the female reproductive costs, I will cite an experiment in which bone demineralization was triggered (Specker, 1994) in lactating mothers who lacked adequate calcium in their body, so that the required amount of calcium in their milk was maintained! Well, this is shocking, but is it really? The body of a female would compromise its own stability so that the infant does not faces malnourishment! This experiment hence clarifies that the biological priorities of a female is not centered at her own longevity, but that of her offspring.

We must hence conclude that the costs of reproduction are as significant for the female as they are for the male.

The aging man
"Last scene of all,
That ends this strange eventful history,
Is second childishness and mere oblivion,
Sans teeth, sans eyes, sans taste, sans everything."

-Shakespeare

Aging is sad, yet believed to be unpreventable. Many biologists believe that aging is a disease, with its own symptoms. Let us study some of the symptoms of aging on brain and the rest of the body-

On brain

It was earlier wrongfully believed that neurogenesis in an adult brain is not possible, which was aimed to explain the cognitive decline attributed with old age. This assumption has quickly been ruled out, yet the question of cognitive decline with aging hovers in the air. What causes it? Why does it happen?

Here are some experiments in this direction:-

1. Loss of stem cells (Siwak-Tapp, 2007): Neurogenesis is done by stem cells at specialized sites in the brain. Although neurogenesis in adults is possible, the number of neurogenesis sites has been shown to decrease with age, thus reducing the supply of new cells with age while the demand for new cells remains, hence creating imbalance and imperfections in the brain over the years. This may be shocking since about *250 million new sperm cells* are manufactured in the body every day almost consistently throughout life. So, why does neurogenesis in *brain* dwindles when testes never stop producing sperm cells? (This sounds similar to the functioning of a corrupt government in a country, which spends such and such amount of money on *useless* schemes but only a small amount on research or education!)
2. Loss of brain volume (A. F. Fotenos, 2005): It has been famously demonstrated that the volume of the brain decreases with age. It is not clear whether this change in volume actually indicates loss of brain cells or simply their shrinkage. Yet, it is to be noted that the decrease in volume itself indicates that the old age brain is not doing well.

The fact that the brain indeed suffers a cognitive decline due to aging has been confirmed in many experiments, which typically involves testing an old brain against younger ones upon some challenging tasks, revealing a loss in the ability of the aged brain to process information quickly, learn new things and solve new type of problems.

Yet, it should be noted that decline in cognitive function is neither necessary nor irreversible for an aging brain, as the health of the brain has been shown to have direct correlation with the lifestyle (Pereira, 2007) of the person. For example, people who live an intellectually stimulating life suffer less brain decline than the others. Similarly, the performance of a brain which is known to have suffered some age related functional decline has been shown to improve on the change of lifestyle, like a change in nutrition, exercise schedule and environment.

These evidences suggest that age related decline in the performance of the brain is preventable, and is simply about the biological priorities of a person and is based on the principle of 'use it or lose it'. This fact has strong implications for the theory of Brahmacharya, as we will be seeing shortly.

On rest of the body

The effect of old age on the body can be summarized in some major points:

- Decrease in body immunity or ability to fight diseases, which causes the onset of many chronic diseases like diabetes, heart diseases, asthma etc,
- Decrease in the ability to repair and maintain the body,
- Decrease in physical strength and muscle mass,
- Loss of organic function, like loss of sight, hearing, sense of coordination etc, and
- Physical degradation like- wrinkling of skin, baldness (in males), graying of hairs, loss of teeth etc.

It should be noted that one need not study the degradation of brain and body *separately*, and we may see them as the result of the same phenomenon. The rate of aging of the brain and body is both decided by lifestyle factors, like presence or absence of intellectually stimulating habits, a good balanced diet and other habits like regular exercise. Hence one can conclude that aging *may* not be the result of some biologically necessary condition, and might instead exist because of some entirely different reasons. We will discuss these ideas in detail shortly.

Works Cited

A. F. Fotenos, S. A. (2005). Normative estimates of cross-sectional and longitudinal brain volume decline in aging and AD. *Neurology* , 1032-1039.

HAMILTON, J. B. (1960). EFFECT OF CASTRATION IN ADOLESCENT AND YOUNG ADULT MALES UPON FURTHER CHANGES IN THE PROPORTIONS OF BARE AND HAIRY SCALP. *The Journal of Clinical Endocrinology & Metabolism* , 1309-1318.

Harcourt, A. H. (1995). Sperm competition: mating system, not breeding season, affects testes size of primates. *Functional Ecology, 468-476.* , 468-476.

James B. Hamilton, P. G. (1969). Mortality and Survival: Comparison of Eunuchs with intact men and women in a Mentally Retarded population. *Journal of Jerontology* , 395-411.

Linda Partridge, D. G. (2005). Sex and Death: What Is the Connection? *Cell* , 461-471.

Mats Olsson, T. M. (1997). Is sperm really so cheap? Costs of reproduction in male adders, Vipera berus. *Proceedings of the royal society B: Biological Sciences* , 455-459.

Min, K. J. (2012). The lifespan of Korean eunuchs. *Current Biology*, 792-793.

Pereira, A. C. (2007). An in vivo correlate of exercise-induced neurogenesis in the adult dentate gyrus. *Proceedings of the National Academy of Sciences*, 5638-5643.

Robertson, O. H. (1961). Prolongation of the life span of kokanee salmon (Oncorhynchus nerka kennerlyi) by castration before beginning of gonad development. *Proceedings of the National Academy of Sciences*, 609-621.

Ruth Thomsen, J. S. (2006). How costly are ejaculates for Japanese macaques? *Primates*, 272-274.

Siwak-Tapp, C. T. (2007). Neurogenesis decreases with age in the canine hippocampus and correlates with cognitive function. *Neurobiology of learning and memory*, 249-259.

Specker, B. L. (1994). Nutritional concerns of lactating women consuming vegetarian diets. *The American Society for Clinical Nutrition*, 1182S-1186S.

Stearns, S. (1976). Life-history tactics: a review of the ideas. *Quarterly review of biology*, 3-47.

Terry W. Snell, C. E. (1977). Lifespan and Fecundity pattern in Rotifers: The cost of reproduction. *Evolution*, 882-890.

Weindruch, R. (1996). The Retardation of Aging by Caloric Restriction: Studies in Rodents and Primates. *Toxicologic pathology*, 742-745.

Part2: The Grand theory of Celibacy

Now it is the time to see how we can explain the 'facts' observed in the experiments we studied in the previous chapter. Please note that the theory that we will be discussing will be non-technical in the sense that we will not be memorizing one million and one difficult scientific names of different enzymes, hormones, chemicals and biological processes. Evidence shows that all the difficulties in all the difficult subjects studied by human beings that excite a few and scares away the rest of us, is only a difficulty very trivial in nature- the difficulty of communication. Take for example, mathematics, and to be more precise, Gauss theorem. It can take an ugly procedure of calculus to prove that spherical planets can be assumed as bodies whose mass is concentrated at their centers, yet, using Gauss's method, the entire mechanics of the situation can be understood by a simple visualization, based on symmetry.

So, what makes the calculus method of it ugly?

The ordinary mind does not understand and is not trained to comprehend and process the symbols used in the calculus method. So, you see, the calculus behind it appears ugly because one does not understands the *meaning* of the symbols. It is as simple and trivial as *that*! For a person who understands what the symbols mean the idea behind calculus is trivial, easy and beautiful.

So, it appears that brain is designed to understand the mysteries of the cosmos, be it through art, physics or mathematics. What the brain is *not* designed for is to convey the sophisticated ideas to each other using ugly and unrelated words, symbols and sounds. Our brain does not think in terms of English or mathematical symbols. The ugliness lies when we have to translate our thoughts into them for the reader or listener, so that the latter can take in the words and convert them back into the original idea. It is a shame that children have to labor so much learning the alphabets, math symbols, biology terms etc, probably ending up giving these things *more* importance than the actual, wordless, formless abstract ideas that the words stand for.

So, we will not be focusing on the difficult biological details that are studied by the experts. Instead of going in the details, we will study the *thermodynamics of biology*, to take an analogy from physics. In physics when we need to study a situation, like a flying airplane, there is too much data involved, like the size, structure and mass of each air molecule colliding with the molecules of the airplane. Instead of going in so much detail, physicists and engineers instead study some macroscopic properties, like air pressure, wind velocity, viscosity, temperature etc to analyze the same situation approximately. This proves to be a practical move, since analyzing the effect due to each molecule would be very difficult.

We will be following a similar procedure while examining the biology behind celibacy over here. Based on the scientific data discussed in the previous chapter, we will try to carve a theory which understands life as a bulk system, without studying the whereabouts and processes at the cellular level. We will go in the details where it is required though, but will generally stick to having a bird eye view to the system, to maintain the readability of this book.

Now, what we want to understand is the biological theory of Brahmacharya, so that the biology reveals to us the true nature of life, and so that we divert our attention from sexual thoughts for a while to pay attention to the other parts of ourselves, the parts that otherwise may be left untouched and unfelt. Truth is delicious. Let nobody be denied truth.

Finally, I put the disclaimer that all scientific theories can be challenged, so if you think that the theory discussed in this book is wrong, kindly do not stay quiet, and write up your opinion to the author through email or at the website, as indicated in the back matter of this book so that we can together consider our arguments. Also, if you agree with the theory or feel like adding something to it, kindly express your opinion at the same place.

So, let us begin...

Do we kill our self in the end, or the circumstances kill us?

Scientists have, for about 150 years, struggled to explain aging. Is it necessary? What causes it?

There are mainly two theories that are aimed to explain the mysteries of why we get old and die. The first one says that aging is *programmed* into us for some benefit, and the other says that it is *caused* by some factors, and is simply the result of our body's inability to remain young. Let us understand these theories one by one.

Programmed theory of aging:

The Programmed theory says that life has evolved in such a way that organism are programmed to die on their own after they reach a specie specific age. And the reason for this is simple- because there is some benefit of getting old.

The following benefits are suggested:

1. Programmed deaths would accelerate the rate of evolution since older organisms would give up the space for the newer ones to evolve, hence passing the torch of development quickly to the newly mutated

organisms, and hence speeding up the process of evolution.
2. Programmed deaths would help in checking overpopulation in the specie. The analogy is brought from our own body, in which, if cells are allowed immortality, they develop into cancerous tumor and eventually cause the death of the organism. So, it is suggested that organisms get old for the same reason- just to check the unchecked growth.

Hence, this theory suggests that there exists an inbuilt mechanism within the organism that stifles its life after a certain age is achieved. So, aging is not just natural, but also *necessary* and *beneficial*. Our death *must* happen in order for our specie to survive. Hence this theory promises little assurance to the people who do not want to grow old.

Non-programmed theory of aging:

Non-programmed theory of aging says that the body ages simply because of its inability to repair and maintain itself. The idea is that the body constantly experiences cellular damages caused by radiation and chemical, microbial and mechanical stress. These constantly occurring damages have to be repaired, and the body's inability to efficiently do it leads to these damages collecting over time, to cause severe problems that ages people and eventually takes them down.

This theory deals with aging as a disease and also considers it a theoretically preventable one.

Now, having seen both the theories of aging, one must note that reasonable objection can be made against both the theory.

Now, I present few objections against the programmed theory of aging through these questions:

1. How can the trait of aging get natural selection in the environment? If aging prevents overpopulation to benefit the entire specie, still the trait of aging must explain how it can benefit an *individual organism* within the specie in order to get natural selection. But as far as we can see, an aging individual has no survival advantage over a non aging one if the trait of aging is preprogrammed on the former just to age and kill it. If the trait of aging exists simply to kill organism in order to reduce the population, how can such an organism which gets weaker and slower over time get natural selection under tight competition against organisms that do not age?

2. Secondly, given that an aging individual has no advantage over a non-aging one, the only possible way through which aging individuals can *still* get naturally selected is if the *non-aging individual* causes their specie to *definitely* get extinct, through mechanism like over population. This will imply that the only way through which life can proceed is through selecting the aging individuals, through the act of chance, since the non-aging ones never let their specie live for long.

   Hence, we will have to provide a *mechanism* through which the non-aging individuals cause the population to get extinct through over population. But *can this really happen?* Will extinction *always* follow over population? It sounds unreasonable to me, because the two words- 'extinction' and 'overpopulation' mean exactly the opposite. History stands as evidence that cannibalism and intra specie violence exists, implying that whenever a population with low mortality becomes dominant, the dwindling resources increase competition and hence mortality within the specie,

hence checking the population. So given a cutting edge competition, violence and cannibalism, can non-aging specie really get over populated, and extinct after that, without stopping at anywhere in between?
3. Also, if older species die just to speed up the process of evolution, then how can one explain the diversity that exists in the lifespan of different organisms on earth? For example, Elephants can live for decades, so why is the lifespan of a mouse just 1-2 years? Maybe because the threat of death to a mouse due to non-aging causes is greater. But then, why does a mouse gets old in its already short lifespan? And also, why does not an elephant accelerate its aging to fetch few extra evolutionary points?
4. If the trait of getting old is programmed into us, how can some physical factors like exercise, nutrition and dietary restriction affect the rate of aging?

Surely, there are some other factors at play which are killing us than the simple programmed genetic suicide!

I have following 2 objections against the non-programmed theory of aging:
1. If aging is really a disease, why has not life mastered it yet? Why has not life adapted to this ultimate threat?
2. Again, how can the *non-programmed theory* of aging explain the diversity that exists in the lifespan of organisms on Earth? Elephant and man age at equal rates, while turtles age very slowly and some jelly fish do not get old at all! Rats age very fast! If an efficient procedure of repair and maintenance is the only thing between an organism and its perennial youth, how can one explain this diversity?

I think that a correct theory to explain aging has to be a mixture of the above two theories. For example, it is absolutely absurd to assume that life has developed a suicidal biological mechanism of aging to check overpopulation, because Darwinian evolution demands that population be checked through competition and the phenomenon of the fittest to survive. If the organisms become philanthropically suicidal, this will imply less competition, less struggle, and a blunt knife of natural selection which fails to select anything, since individuals would be dying on their own, without the necessity of their weakness killing them.

So, a big question is staring at us. Why does aging exist at all? I have a theory- aging must have immediate benefits! Aging, through some mechanism, must *directly* benefit the individual who gets old! Given two individuals, with one who ages and other who does not, the life of the one who gets old must be *more* successful and productive! Yes, I am absolutely aware of what I am claiming! In spite of the weaknesses associated with aging, in spite of everything, the individual who ages can defeat the individual who does not by getting natural selection. Given a population which does not ages, eventually the trait of aging will appear as mutation and will attain natural selection, but not to check over population, but to simply increase reproductive success…!

I am sane. But I will reveal no more for now. Let us understand this theory from a proper angle. So we will get back to this shortly!

The life history theory and the suicidal world

After studying the experiments in part 1 of this book, we have reached at the place where we start understanding their actual meaning. For this purpose, let me summarize the findings of the experiments in a short list:

1. There exists an inverse relationship between the lifespan and fecundity of all organisms.
2. Castration increases the lifespan of an organism, hence corroborating the statement (1).
3. Reproduction is a costly life process, hence corroborating the statement (1) and (2) as stated above.
4. Aging is a degradation of life, yet rate of degradation can be controlled by some environmental factors like nutrition and exercise etc. This implies that the process of degradation seems to be flexible, and not a pre-programmed and unpreventable one.

What we now have to do is to weave a complete biological theory which satisfactorily explains all the above facts and does not contradicts with some of the already established theories in biology, like the theory of evolution, without explicitly stating the reason for the same.

Such a theory already exists in biology. Its name is- Life History Theory.

According to life history theory:

1. The resources available to any living system in natural condition are limited. This is the same as saying that there exists a physical limit to the energy that an organism can eat, store in his body and process within a given limit of time.
2. Organism must carry out some life processes like repair and maintenance of their body, reproduction, cognitive function, maintenance of a certain amount of muscular mass for strength in order to survive etc.
3. All these life processes must have cost attached to them, which is individually significant and comparable.
4. In order to fulfill a certain life process, resources must be supplied towards it, and the same resource cannot be used to fulfill some other life process.

5. For the above reasons, a measurable *tradeoff* mechanism between the life processes must exist when it comes to allotting resources towards them. For example, more resources invested towards reproduction must be achieved by '*diverting*' some energy which was earlier going towards the other life process. Hence, inhibiting a life process from being expressed will directly increase the amount of energy available towards the other life processes.
6. The proportion of energy that an organism distributes towards different life processes is decided by evolutionary as well as environmental priorities of the organism. If you do not use a given life process, you start allocating less resources towards it.

The fact that reduced fecundity in rats induces an increase in their lifespan indicates a kind of inverse relationship between these traits- 'reproduction' and 'repair and maintenance of body'. It is as if these two traits *compete* for the resources within the body. The idea is that staying alive and reproducing are both costly processes for an organism.

Staying alive is costly because an organism has to constantly repair the radiation and chemical, mechanical and microbial damages that is being brought to the cells in order to stay alive. So, old age *happens* when a large number of such small cellular damages collect over time to finally strangulate the organism into death.

Reproduction, on the other hand, is costly too, as we have already seen in the experiments discussed in part 1.

We left the question of 'why we age' half unanswered in the last section. The complete answer is that we age because our priority to reproduce compromises our priorities to repair and maintain our body, hence causing a gradual degradation in our body system. The idea is that reproduction saps our body out of the resources, and our body consciously lets this happen, and makes us gradually disappear from the world by slowly becoming a corpse as we age.

I can see that you have got objections to this latest development of the matter! Well, kindly be patient, because I have not yet stated the complete mechanism. Also we will soon arrive at this same conclusion from different point of views, which is sure to convince you!

Now, notice how this theory combines the *programmed theory of aging* with the *non-programmed* one. Our body indeed commits a suicide, as demanded by the programmed theory, but the mechanism of suicide or aging is not biologically wired into us, but is instead simply the result of *neglect* of repair and maintenance of the body against constantly occurring damages, by directing the resources towards reproduction. If the mechanism behind aging was wired in us, dietary restriction would not slow aging as simply as it *does* slow it down.

A compromised repair and maintenance of our body, you may notice, is the condition demanded by the non-programmed theory of aging. We age because aging has benefit, and we age because we do not repair the constantly occurring cellular damage! Hence, the two theories are unified!

But why do we do it? Why do we direct all resources towards reproduction and compromise the repair and maintenance? Notice how the benefit of faster aging is nothing but an increased fecundity in the organism, hence increasing the reproductive success of the individual over lifetime, and hence giving an individual who gets old a direct benefit over his peers who do not, because reduction in rate of aging comes with reduction in fecundity, as we have already seen in part 1 of this book. Notice that the two processes- reproduction and aging are interlinked, so if an individual is aging faster, he is simultaneously gaining reproductive vigor in return! This is 'the benefit' of aging that I was talking about. *Aging benefits the very organism that chooses to get old!* So are you beginning to see the pieces of the jig-saw puzzle group together?

But there is one missing piece, the factor that acts as a propeller to this theory. Without a propeller, this theory, which is just a logically consistent collection of sentences as yet, would not be able to move at all! This theory, as tells your intuition, is right now incomplete. We need a *reason* for the effects of this theory to become as dramatic and significant as they are. We need a propeller.

Even the worst skeptics who have followed our logic till now will agree that this theory *does make sense*, even if the effect of tradeoff between fecundity and 'repair and maintenance' in the body may *not be significant*. For example, the skeptics may claim that the effect of this tradeoff is not so significant to cause old age, but they must agree that the tradeoff, however insignificant, does exists. Once they agree to this, we will eventually make them agree to the rest of the theory!

So, the propeller that empowers our theory is the *natural death* rate of an organism, beyond that of aging.

All organism, whether they age or not, *have to die*, as caused by accidents, like drowning in flood, getting electric shock, dying out of mechanical shock from rocks falling from sky etc. This simple fact *propels* the above theory because if an organism tunes his rate of aging such that his life expectancy *matches* that of his non-aging peer facing same threats of life, then both of them will end up with almost *identical* life expectancy, yet one of them, the one who *ages*, will have *more* kids, just because he was wise enough to sap his body by an *extra* amount in order to have few *extra* number of *extra* healthy kids!

Suppose a non aging animal population dies in 10 years on average. Now suppose a clever mutant among the specie decides to compromise the repair and maintenance process of his body in order to obtain few *extra* pangs of energy for reproduction, so that his body starts to age, but in such a manner that he dies, out of old age, somewhere near 'the 10 years mark'. So, what did the aging animals lose? Maybe a year from his life span... But what did he gain? Increased sexual function! How can we prove that there was a net gain? We can prove this by examining their *dead bodies*. The non-aging animal's dead body would be as healthy and robust as you can imagine, simply because he did not age. But what will happen to the 'healthy' dead body of this non-aging miser now? It is of no more use to the animal, and all the energy that went in maintaining its health and young age is now wasted! So, is it not logical to propose that a mathematically more efficient life strategy for such mortal organism will be to scrape and erode their own health for *more* reproduction, since reproduction is the thing that makes *offspring* that outlive your mortal self and make you immortal? Is not aging the consequence of simple mathematical strategy, the result of game theory? Is not the individual who tunes his lifespan through aging to match it to that of his non-aging peer being wiser by investing *some more* on reproduction and *some less* on repair and maintenance of the body? Did we not observe how the lactating female let her bones demineralize for her offspring? Are not our 'healthy' sexual expressions *tuned* to be biologically excessive, whatever be the resources available to us?

Do you get the logic? If not, do not worry, because we will be discussing this more from different perspectives. But it is important over here to see why I called the natural death rate of organisms from causes beyond aging the propeller which drives this theory into importance. If the death rate due to external causes was insignificant, then effectively repairing and maintaining the body would become completely necessary, just because low death rate would mean a long life to live and look forward to. But as soon as the death rate due to external causes becomes significant, the organisms who decide to age in a calculated manner end up having a biologically more productive life, increasing their chances of getting natural selection. Because, if our chances of dying are large, why should we waste energy in preserving our body? Why would you spend thousands in repairing a phone which is old and is likely to die soon?

This Biological theory seems to be giving Brahmacharya a direct nod of approval, but the question is, how significant is this effect caused by tradeoff between lifespan and fecundity? There are many criticisms that this theory will have to bear at this point. I will name a few of them:

1. If old age and death is caused by neglect of cellular damage, will eating a little more prevent old age, since in that case we would have increased the *input* of resources in the body? In a same way, will Taoist practice of 'injaculation' be beneficial to those who are concerned about loss of energy during ejaculation? Also, why can't taking some nutrient supplements help one regain the claimed loss of health during sex?
2. If tradeoff between resources used for reproduction and life span exists, why should it be *important*? In other words, there are so many life processes executed by the body, like doing intellectual work, maintaining muscle mass etc. Why should resources invested in reproduction be *the extra* dangerous one? Why should reproduction be the *one* always standing in the way of the youth of a person? This is a good question. Why should we give *special* attention to reproduction, which is just another life process

needing resources? Why cannot we remain young along with having an active reproductive life?
3. Why should the resources available for repair and maintenance of the body be always *shorter* than the resources required to efficiently carrying on the same thing? Also, why should the resources used/wasted in reproduction be always sufficient to make up the deficiency as noted in the last sentence? In other words, why is life tuned so that you will grow old no matter what resources are available, until and unless you practice celibacy? What is the sense in that?

Three imaginary worlds

Imagine that there are three parallel worlds- world A, B and C where different colonies of biologically identical human beings exist in exactly similar life conditions.

Imagine that in world A, people *never* grow old, and they never reproduce because body resources available to them is just a little bit more than what is required to repair and maintain their body with 100% efficiency. People in world 'A' use the extra energy by doing creative things, like weaving baskets in their free time.

In the world B, people again *never* grow old, but they use their 'extra body resources' through reproduction. So, they have a little sex, every now and then, because they cannot have more as their first priority is staying young and they hence cannot compromise the repair and maintenance of their body.

In the third world- world C, the people are completely sexually inclined, and reproduction is one of their top priorities. Hence, their repair and maintenance system gets compromised, and they are vulnerable to getting old, so tuned that their average lifespan is not much less than that of the people from world A and B. (Note again that although the people from world A and B do not age, they *do* have an average lifespan!)

So, what is your bet? Which one of these civilizations will outlive the rest two, and which of the civilization will get extinct first?

It is an easy guess that people of world A will get extinct first, because they have no plans for having children. So, although they do not age, they will die all the same, eventually. Yet, people from world A would be the most creative, since they invested the most amount of energy towards it, and they will leave some beautiful hand-woven baskets behind them as they die!

Now, since the people in world B also do not age, they will have the exactly same pattern of mortality as those in world A. Yet the people in the world B would leave behind few children, implying that they do not get extinct *that* easily.

Finally, the people in the world C will have a distinct pattern of mortality, consisting partially of natural causes of death and partially of age related mortality. Hence although the overall death rate will be highest, the reproductive output of world C will be gigantic (given that they are mathematical enough to tune their rate of aging to that sweet spot which gives them the most net benefit), because they had been diverting the energy allotted for the repair and maintenance process of their body towards reproduction.

So the question is who, between B and C, has the best life strategy and is most likely to get natural selection during evolution?

The answer is clearly C. C's strategy is the best, since it has the mathematical benefit of *committing calculated suicide*. Compromising the process of repair and maintenance of the body is an act of committing suicide. Since the organism would die of causes beyond aging all the same, the natural selection of the trait favoring suicidal tendency seems obvious, because self triggered compromise in repair and maintenance of the body comes with increased reproductive success. In other words, every time an old man dies out of diabetes roughly at the same age at which he would have otherwise died trying to climb a tree in a hypothetical situation of zero aging, his life must be considered a more successful one, since having allowed himself to get old, the old man bought some reproductive success without compromising his overall life expectancy!

Graph 4: Population survival pattern in an aging and non-aging population

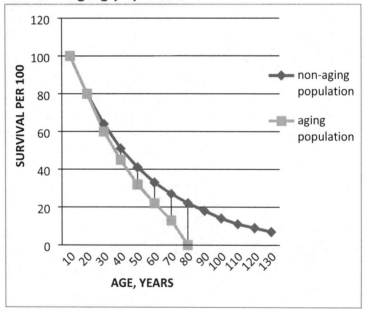

Hence according to our theory, a finely tuned rate of aging *aimed* to kill the organism at some specie specific age is a better life strategy than to not to age at all, as far as reproductive success is concerned. Moreover, this specie specific age is nothing but roughly the life expectancy of the same species in zero aging conditions. In other words, even if the organism does not ages, he will have a life expectancy attached to his living conditions, depending upon the risk of predation, injuries, calamity etc. Hence if the organism fine tunes his bodily aging to match this life expectancy, it will suffer minimal loss in its lifespan while at the same time gaining evolutionary benefit through enhanced reproductive success.

This is the same as if you were given, let us say, 1 million dollar, with the condition that any amount of cash that you do not spend within a week will be confiscated. Hence although normally you would not 'kill' so much cash in so little time, now you are prompted to make the best of the situation in the given time. So what should you do? You keep the cash *as long as possible* with yourself, while 'finely tuning' the expenditure to match the 'deadline'. You spend 1 million dollars in a week! You *kill* the money slowly, with 'age', in order to 'buy' 'something' which can *outlive* the barrier of 1 week imposed on the cash. You are making the cash *live longer* by *spending* it!

Do you see the analogy?

So, this thought experiment suggests that if there exist two organisms, one like B, who has reproduction, but not at the cost of harming its own youth by neglecting other life processes; and the other like C, the one which scrapes his body's survival necessities selflessly just for the sake of higher sexual success, then the evolution will choose C over B, B's reproductive moderation becoming its weakness. Do you see why I called reproduction as not being a fancy activity in the Introduction? There is *too* much at stake. The organism runs the risk of *death* and *old age* to accomplish reproduction. The organism *scrapes* its body resources till the last mathematical limit, to attain a balance which ensures a highly sexual life with as much longevity as possible, and no more.

This argument explains why turtles live till centuries while an adult mayfly dies in 2 days. The difference is caused by the difference in their mortality rate or the risk to their life. A miser mayfly that does not pour *all* of its accumulated life energy towards its first copulation and instead prefers to stay young would die all the same, maybe within the next few hours, out of accidents! In turtles, the risks are not *that* high, hence they enjoy longer lives, without caring about overpopulation, simply because no specie worries about over-population. Over population is like an unattainable motive for any specie.

The cost of dead bodies

We can come to the same result by another angle, namely the resources wasted by the world B and C in the form of dead bodies to explain aging.

In the world B, all the deaths happen on young, healthy and robust people, because nobody gets old there. Hence, B wastes a lot of resources in the form of dead bodies.

On the contrary, in the world C the old people are already nearly corpses, and mere shadow of their former self. Their bones and tendons are visible, their brain has shrunken and degraded, their skins have wrinkled and their eyes, ears and major internal organ are at the verge of failure. The people in world C instead prefer to sap the final drops of life out of them, putting it into reproduction, hence minimizing the resources that would be lost in the form of dead body.

The difference is quite remarkable. Our world is the world C. We are sexually excessive, whatever one may like to think, and we tend to minimize loss of resources through dead bodies. Our old people are corpse for a purpose. Our tendency to age has a benefit. This is the most efficient strategy in the game of life.

We can sense a complete theory of Brahmacharya somewhere nearby.

Our logic till now

So now that we have given time and thought about the arguments given in the book, let us add a summary of the arguments to make a strong theory:

- Every life process involves cost for organisms. Hence, processes like repair and maintenance, reproduction have to deal with competition for resources when the resource is limited. And by the way, resource *is* limited in real life.
- Even if repair and maintenance of body is made 100% effective, people will die, and will have a finite and even short life expectancy, caused by high amount of competition among different organisms from same and different species in struggle to survive.
- Since life expectancy is short, reproduction is an organism's only ticket to eternity, the idea behind reproduction being to produce as many copies of you as possible, so that extinction of the population is avoided.
- But reproduction is no fancy activity. It is strongly linked with chances of survival; hence organisms must scrape their body resources and compromise their process of 'repair and maintenance' as much as they can, so that their life expectancy remains roughly unchanged while their reproductive output increases. Their life expectancy will remain roughly the same, I will point out once again, because earlier they were dying out of accidents, but now they will be dying out

of their own lack of interest in remaining immune to degradation.
- Hence, organisms avoid wastage of resources in the form of dead bodies by consciously letting themselves become a corpse before they die by simply ignoring body damages. Also, it should hence be noted that reproduction is not like other life processes when we see its resource consumption. Reproduction is like a giant with infinite appetite at a dinner-party, asking the other guests to eat only as much as they must, and leave the rest for him. Reproduction is like a full stop. If you use it liberally, it will always end the sentence. Reproduction is a suicide mechanism employed by organisms. Reproduction is one of the highest priorities in the life of an organism, since the life of an organism has a definite and even short life expectancy. It seems that every organism is a cunning mathematician, and it cuts its own throat for the sake of logic and optimum strategy of survival.

Now, I would like answer the questions that were raised in the previous section:

Question 1: If old age and death is caused by neglect of cellular damage, will eating a little more prevent old age, since in that case we would have increased the input of resources in the body? In a same way, will Taoist practice of 'injaculation' be beneficial to those who are concerned about loss of energy during ejaculation? Also, why can't taking some nutrient supplements help one regain the claimed loss of health during sex?

Answer: The effect of eating a little more or increasing the body resources will depend upon the fact whether one will also be able to process the extra food or not. In a normal individual, there exists a weight ratio height limit that a person can have and still remain healthy. The effect of over feeding tends to be unhealthy and can cause obvious survival limitations caused by obesity. Hence the resource limitation of the body is not completely dependent upon how much we *eat*, but also on how much our body is prepared to *process* the food in a given time.

Graph 5: Relationship between lifespan and fecundity of organism under various resource constraints

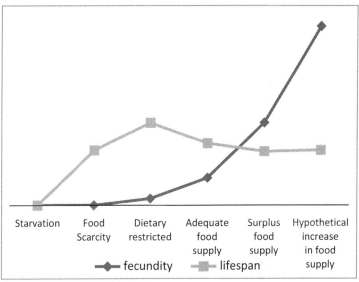

Yet, in a biologically hypothetical situation where resources available are indeed increased so slowly that the organism is able to biologically adapt to the increased resources by bringing forth some structural changes in his body in order to assimilate the increased resources, and given that the change in the structure does not changes the mortality rate of the organism, (which is only an approximation because increased resources should increase the size of the organism and decrease the rate of mortality by some amount) then the rate of aging and fecundity can be studied as a function of resources available, as shown in the graph.

One can notice that given a mortality rate, the lifespan of a non aging organism is limited, hence indicating that once, through adequate dietary intake, this natural life expectancy is achieved, any further increase in resources has minuscule effects on rate of aging, while it increases the fecundity indefinitely.

Hence, short answer to the above objection is that if we somehow increase the resources available to us in order to check our aging, the aging will not slow down. Instead, the resources will go down the sink of reproduction and other immediate life processes that determine our productivity. The reason is simply that reproduction becomes the first priority of a healthy and well fed organism, and because the organism simply does not wants to slow down aging, for a simple *non-inclination* towards living longer! The sexual inclinations prevent us from being young forever!

This should help us in answering why the Taoists have it wrong. The process of injaculation can be seen as an attempt to conserve the energy from getting wasted during ejaculation. But extra nutrients do not have any effect on the lifespan of an individual, given, of course, that the individual is taking a healthy diet. It is the *priority* of the body which comes in the way to of its health, not energy available. Given any finite supply of energy, the best strategy is to invest all the extra parts of it on present life processes requirements, because storing for future is not an option, because in a real threatening environment there does not exists a long stable future.

It is worth noting that if the supply of energy is somehow made infinite and mechanism be provided so that the organism can easily assimilate all of it, then we will arrive at the concept of the 'Darwinian Giant'. Darwinian Giant is a term which refers to a hypothetical organism that has no life threats, and has infinite supply of energy, such that it can keep on growing indefinitely in size and having indefinite number of off springs. It should also be noted that a Darwinian Giant has not yet been found, and if one existed, it would be easy to spot owing to its large size.

Getting back to the argument against Taoist practice of injaculation, it is worth noting one implication- that although ejaculation in males is costly, the hype that tries to glorify the cost of semen is certainly misguided. It is here that the supporters of celibacy close their ears to all reasonable arguments against it and those who argue against it stare at the supporters with frustration and helplessness, and all debates end. Is ejaculation really so costly that, nutritionally speaking, it can explain all the benefits that are associated with Brahmacharya? If yes, then what if one decides to take some nutrition supplements to regain the loss in health?

The correct resolution has already been discussed. Reproduction incurs a continuous and strenuous cost upon the body. The costs do not come in discrete packets, to put the idea forward with humor, when a man is ejaculating. So, one should not 'count' the number of ejaculations, and calculate its frequency over time, to compare how much 'celibate' one is. Instead, the cost associated with reproduction is more metabolic in nature, and is always going on.

Every moment, a part of our metabolism is recruited to maintain our sexual fertility, and a part of the mind is subconsciously busy plotting the plans for future potential sexual opportunities. Psychologists put this idea more elegantly by saying that everything we do in life, however innocent the act be, has some subconscious sexual intention hidden behind it. It may appear an exaggeration, and maybe it is, but more or less, it is true.

Reproduction is a life process, and it is one of the most important one. And the idea behind Brahmacharya is to carry the mind and body to a higher plane of existence, and to reduce the subconscious investment of the body towards reproduction, not through conscious repression of sexual thoughts, but through sublimation. You want to divert your body priorities from reproduction? Raise yourself to the intellectual plane... Go solve an open math problem unsolved for last 400 years... Go paint some canvasses with the passion competing Van Gogh's... The concept of sublimation is very simple. It happens very naturally. There exist more 'philosophical' books on this aspect of Brahmacharya, so I would dig no deeper.

I will mention one last thing. You might have noticed that I have not actually provided an exact metabolic mechanism through which reproduction as a life process incurs cost upon the body. Actually, I do not know of any such mechanism, this being a biologically complicated topic to study and establish. Then how do I know that such a mechanism exists? Because we have already *seen* many experiments that show that reproduction is costly for the organism. And this proves that a mechanism to incur such costs *must* exist.

But other than this, the existence of such a mechanism also gives rise to a beautiful and self-consistent theory of trade-off of resources between life processes. And since truth is beautiful, we have another argument in our support.

Question 2: If tradeoff between resources used for reproduction and life span exists, why should it be important? In other words, there are so many life processes executed by the body, like doing intellectual work, maintaining muscle mass etc. Why should resources invested in reproduction be the extra dangerous one? Why should reproduction be the one always standing in the way of the youth of a person? This is a good question. Why should we give special attention to reproduction, which is just another life process needing resources? Why cannot we remain young along with having an active reproductive life?

Answer: We have already discussed this. As we can see in the graph above, the reproductive life process becomes more important than other once the organism reaches a state of being well fed. In animal world, it is seen that fecundity of organisms increases if a stable and nourishing environment in made available. This is because in a stable environment, there already exists an upper limit to the longevity of the organisms, and hence the only ticket to eternity is through reproduction.

So, as we have discussed, the resources spent in reproduction causes a calculated rate of aging in the organisms to increase lifetime productivity. Hence, we can say that reproduction is a special kind of life process. No amount of reproduction is enough, if it can be had.

Question 3: Why should the resources available for repair and maintenance of the body be always shorter than the resources required to efficiently carrying on the same thing? Also, why should the resources used/wasted in reproduction be always sufficient to make up the deficiency as noted in the last sentence? In other words, why is life tuned so that you will grow old no matter what resources are available, until and unless you practice celibacy? What is the sense in that?

Answer: This is because given any supply of resources and any death rate, it is the best strategy for the organism to slowly erode itself to old age to increase its lifelong productivity and reduce the costs in the form of dead bodies, without altering its lifespan by a large amount.

Breaking the silence on Brahmacharya

I would like to point out that most of the theory I have been discussing till now is not my own original discovery. I have been mostly repeating the conclusions of many biological theorists and experimentalists. Yet, when we try to find out a serious scientific theory on Brahmacharya, we find none! Brahmacharya is today what it was thousands of years ago… a philosophical idea, notoriously mystical, completely discarded by doctors, scientists and society as superstition. In fact, celibacy is a taboo in the world today, with many people simply afraid of the hypothetical health concerns of not masturbating on daily basis!

So, the question is, why has not anyone tried to develop a complete and serious theory of Brahmacharya based on the available scientific facts as yet? I have 2 theories in this direction. Let us examine them:

- All scientific beliefs in society are influenced not just by truth, but also by what people *want* to believe. The common man in society is a scientific layman, even if he is educated. To have an updated and detailed view on science, he either needs to conduct research on his own or read popular science materials. Hence, what a society believes depends upon what the popular scientific literature contains. Be it time travel or artificial intelligence, the society is educated by popular science authors- those who publish the books, magazines, or run the websites. Now, these authors… these experts who act as an interpreter between people and the actual scientific research, are business centric people. Instead of telling the most important scientific knowledge of the time, they prefer to tell the things that would *interest* the common people the most. Hence, we have popular culture telling people to fully express their sexual instincts, to masturbate to prevent heart disease and to have at least 21 orgasms a month to live a socially healthy life! Now imagine what will happen if an author actually goes on to tell people that their sexual activities is making them old, and bringing them to a decline that they subconsciously seem to desire. The result will be that people will feel uncomfortable, scornful and would shun such texts, even if these are backed up with solid logic and experimental evidences. Hence people seem to desire ignorance, as truth can be horrible, scary and disturbing sometimes. But a correct approach to truth is to examine it with your own perspective and consider its consequences, whatever they may be.

- Secondly, the reason why there are beliefs supporting health benefits of sexual indulgence is that people, even experts, like to make counter intuitive statements to look intelligent, sophisticated and learned. I will explain why I am saying this. There is a unanimous opinion on the internet that masturbation is healthy, especially for the heart, as it helps burn cholesterol! It has been advised in many an 'informed' articles that masturbating once every day is the healthy way to kill fat and become slim! Also, there exists a widely cited medical belief that sexual activities do *not* cause any fatigue and tiredness in a person, and will instead cheer people up and make them stronger.

All these opinions are completely non-intuitive and believed *precisely* for that reason. Drawing an analogy, Einstein impressed the world and became a hero by saying counterintuitive things like- time passes at different rates for different people, length contracts as one moves and gravity is caused by curvature of space-time. People get *impressed* by counter intuitive ideas, and although Einstein appears to be correct, not everyone is. So do not believe an unbelievable idea just because it appears unbelievable. Somebody might be trying to impress and show you that they are cleverer. *Ask* them about their source of information, and *check* the source.

So from here, I will extend the logic developed through these pages to a fully fledged modern scientific theory of Brahmacharya.

The scientific theory of Brahmacharya

If we think about the nature of life around us, we will notice a cycle of being born and giving birth, and not just that, but a *passion* for being born and giving birth to many others. If we think of this carefully, it looks very boring.

I always wanted to become a physicist as a child (I am not a biologist, by the way!), but it irritated me when people described what a physicist did. They told me- first you patiently study physics and then you become a professor and join a prestigious college and build a good academic career. I have since then realized that becoming a professor is indeed first priority and dream come true for any physicist. But, for a person that I am, who does not likes teaching, I saw no point in this- learning physics, just to teach the same to others…! What is the point in this circular way of living?

Same logic goes for being born and then ardently pursuing sexual impulse in the name of love and acceptance and then giving birth and becoming nearly a corpse out of old age in the process. Well, of course there is mathematical logic behind why we get old, but there are so many other kinds of interesting mathematical domains awaiting discovery… what about them? Old age kills a mathematician, a physicist, an artist, a philosopher, everyone! Is sex the only thing important in evolution?

Most of our evolutionary theories consider sexual success the first priority of organism. But this is hardly true since evolution, I think, has now risen higher than just sexuality. Organism has become conscious, has developed the understanding required to distinguish between the mind and the brain. Just sex is not responsible for success of human being as specie... The credit also goes to our desire and ability to explore our surrounding in a scientific way. Reproduction is one method to ensure survival, but it is as important as that and no more. Without science, without curiosity, we would be nowhere where we currently are. But are we currently at a special place? Yes, of course! We are at the brink of earth; we have started jumping, freeing our self from its daunting gravity for the first time, sending probes into outer space. We have built strong telescopes that probe the heart of the cosmos, trying to read its secrets. We have developed frameworks, scientific ideas that have enabled us to study in detail the world of the tiny, sub atomic particles, and we are still studying. We have developed mathematical ideas, the string of logic that has revealed to us many magical gems...

We have come far away from being mere sexually centric beings, so far away that even we don't realize this yet. This world surely is not simply about reproduction. Far away into time, there will come a moment when this speck in the universe, this blue planet, will be smashed into pieces by foreign disturbance. Yes, such time will come! And then, at that time, only bacteria will survive. Sex will not help us then no matter how intensely we pursue it! Sex has no power on asteroids. Science has. Science will help us. We NEED to understand this cosmos, quickly! The outer space is horribly hostile, and we don't stand a chance to survive as specie if we don't understand it, scientifically. If we don't, extinction of life is certain. We need to evade the inevitable. Sexual reproduction was an old strategy in life, used by cats and dogs to multiply. We have risen higher; we have left that old school... If we are still hanging to it every inch, then we are making fools of our self... I think that a person is intellectually pathetic if he or she gives sex a cosmic status in life... the rules of the game, the rules of Darwinian revolution is changing, and life is worth fighting for, and truth is worth being sought...

I would finally like to warn the readers about Celibacy. One should not follow Celibacy just for the sake of following it! You cannot jump your way out of this well. Something must pull you from outside. If you try to jump, your act is meaningless, and you would end up injuring yourself, mentally... Find a *reason* why you need the benefits of Celibacy, and seek the *reason*, not Celibacy. Do not try to 'control' sexual impulse. Rise above it!

Our Body has been wired with sexuality. If you try to re-wire the biological system, just like Mahatma Gandhi was trying to do, by denying its existence, this will cause a lot of struggle. Instead, try to gain biological benefit. Actually, sexuality is not the only wiring present in the body. There are wires regulating curiosity as well. Try to promote the other wires, and the sexual wires will simply go to the background...

Some questions against Brahmacharya:

Do you really think that Celibacy can stop aging?
The answer to this question is complicated. And at present, I can only give an approximate answer.

Assuming complete optimism, yes, celibacy can stop aging. I have already discussed situations that experimentally *demonstrate* the inverse relation between rate of reproduction and lifespan of an organism. So it is clear beyond any shadow of doubt that Celibacy has anti-aging effects.

I have shown how castration tends to increase lifespan as well. I have already argued that any increase in lifespan indicates an increase in the efficiency of repair and maintenance of the body. We discussed the life history theory and the trade off of energy between life processes which is exactly what the results of dietary restriction was based upon. The readers are advised to study these arguments once again if they like.

Hence, all these arguments and experimental data lead us invariably to one conclusion- That celibacy *necessarily* slows down aging in an organism.

But an interesting objection would be- Why did not celibacy *stop* aging in any of the above experiments?

And the short answer is- I do not know why. But I can give some suggestions to possible answer.

Firstly, if celibacy does stop aging, how would we know it? After all, organisms will die all the same, of external causes. The fact is- the non-aging individual in the data also *has* an 'average' age. So, I would repeat that an increase in lifespan of an organism even by a small amount indicates a much larger decrease in rate of aging, because even if the rate of aging becomes zero, the organisms would have only a finite increase in average lifespan. So, the relationship between increase in lifespan and change in rate of aging is not linear.

Secondly, there is a possibility that our body is *intrinsically* suicidal, and that compromising lifespan to increase present productivity is a preferred life strategy, no matter what be the 'type' of productivity we are talking about- Sexual productivity or intellectual.

Many people may not believe it, but an intellectual fellow has to 'burn' his mind in order to look for new ideas that change the world. For example, Nikola Tesla was known to sleep just 2 hours every day! And this was the guy who wanted to make electricity flow *through* air, even though we now know that such a thing might not be practical/safe. But the point is not that. The point is about having a vision and putting all that you have into it. And Tesla did that.

Let's take another example. It is known that after strenuous workout or sports activity, athletes become prone to infection for several days due a temporary decrease in their natural immunity. This not only demonstrates that a trade-off of resources between physical overload and immunity exists, but also that the body is 'okay' with compromising health to boost temporary productivity. Athletes cannot afford to shy away from workout *just* because it temporarily compromises their immunity. If they do, they will be left behind in the competition of life!

So it seems that we need to take the theory of priorities and trade-off of resources within the body based upon our priorities a bit more seriously, and accept the fact that every moment this mechanism is working in the background and continuously putting an upper limit to the amount of life we can afford to live without getting left behind in this competition of the fittest to survive…

So, according to this suggestion, reproductive costs *may* only get *replaced* by other demanding life processes during celibacy, like intellectual or social work, and hence may result in overall aging. But even at its darker side, this clearly means that celibacy is a process of changing the priorities of one's life to things that may matter more, and in the process, may hold the key to gaining access to insights and achievements in one's desired field as has never been realized before. So, even at its worst, the philosophy of celibacy gives to a person the opportunity to attain some potential that would not be otherwise accessible to anyone.

As a last note, I would like to emphasize that although in this answer I entertain the possibility that celibacy may not be completely able to stop aging, I am not really sure about this. For example, it seems reasonable to believe that if one removes sexual demands from the metabolism of a person, then the body may instinctually try to 'preserve' the *self* by boosting the immunity. Reproduction is nothing but a chosen strategy by life to achieve eternity. Can it be that removing reproduction from the scene may trigger plan B in the body- to protect the present form of the self the best it can, through enhanced repair and maintenance, now that there is no scope of reproduction.

Maybe, celibacy coupled with a healthy life style can stop aging. Reminds me of *the monk* from Robin Sharma's book...

If Brahmacharya can stop aging, why has not there ever been a non aging celibate?
This question is related to the previous one, and all the discussions of the previous section apply to this answer as well. But some other attempts to answer this question should go like:

- Celibacy stops aging, and since aging is a slow process, a non-aging individual in society might never get astonished looks in the same way as growing children getting taller do not get astonished looks from their parents every day. This is because the process of getting tall, getting old and the process of *not* getting old, are all very slow ones. Hence if people observe a given *non-aging* individual every day, they will not get astonished on any particular day, and their astonishment will get divided over years to become mere admiration towards the individual. On the other hand, if a *stranger* observes the non-aging individual, he will not be astonished because he will assume that the man is *actually* young.

- A celibate person may never reach middle ages to become an object of astonishment. For example, a person who experiences negligible aging will still be subjected to risks and death, and the mortality rate will also tend to increase in a celibate because with youthfulness comes desire to take risks, which obviously kills. So, the purpose of Brahmacharya is not to live a long life, but to live a satisfactorily happy and adventurous life.

Even celibates may experience aging if they do not take care of themselves. For example, celibacy is not a self contained cure to aging. To stop aging, one needs to meditate, speculate, do exercises or yoga, follow a healthy hygienic life and eat a nutritious diet and take adequate rest.

A small clarification

Readers might have noticed that in this book, although I advocate celibacy, I do not provide any firm biological mechanism through which it would supposedly benefit a person.

For example, in order to technically prove what I claim, specialized experiments are needed in this direction. One also needs to study thousands of people. Celibacy itself makes its study nearly impossible on real subjects because it is a very abstract concept, and not equivalent to semen retention, although experiments about semen retention themselves are quite hard to find, and do not involve a retention period of more than 2 weeks.

Also, one needs to solve many unanswered questions on how human body 'works' in order to answer this question about celibacy.

So, what exactly *did* I try to do in this book?

I did what a good theorist does. I have put before you a theory which fits all the known results in this direction. As I have mentioned before, the theory mentioned in this book is not my own creation (up to a certain level). For example, Life History theory, and its modified versions, is mainstream biological theories. It is generally accepted that our body has to make crucial trade-off decisions between present (re)productivity and future longevity. This small theory 'explains' increase in lifespan in dietary restriction scenario. There are many other detailed experimental observations, like increase in immunity under dietary restriction conditions that can be perfectly explained under the life history theory.

So in this book, I did two interesting things. First, I brought this topic before common people. Before stumbling upon this subject by accident, I myself was completely unaware about Life History Theory, so I am assuming the same about the general reader.

Secondly, I made few bold conclusions, at the risk of being proven wrong, or ridiculed.

I will like to explain the last part. Go to a medical website for some advice about any medical condition. At the end of any informative article you will find a casual warning- "This article should not be considered as a medical advice. It is for general reference only. You should follow your doctor's advice." This message invariably exists, explicitly or implicitly, in many of the articles I have seen out there. The intention of such message is simple- "Although these medical advice is best according to my knowledge, follow it at your own risk."

Just think about it- if a person had the time and money to visit a doctor at the appearance of every odd symptom, why would they go to these medical websites for advice? Hence the role of any medical article should be to state bold conclusions like- "if you get a red pimple on your arm, do not worry. Ask anybody, they don't worry. The chances that it will develop into cancer are negligible". But instead, the websites would say- "although most pimples in many people heal on their own, you should go see a doctor".

Hence it seems it is okay to state facts in the world, but not their conclusions. Because conclusions are small sentences that have the capability of holding all the facts of a book, hence making the facts easily detectable if they are false.

What I mean is, in this book, the short message or conclusion would be- 'we get old because of our more immediate reproductive priorities.' A blunter conclusion would be- 'Sex causes old age'. I can already imagine people scoffing at the latter statement, but if you read research articles in this field, related to life history theory and dietary restriction experiments for example, you will realize that this is what all of them implicitly hint towards. So the question is- why don't biologists state a similar laconic conclusion? ...Because there is a risk of being proven wrong.

Now, getting back to the reason why I started this section. There is another reason why biologists do not state laconic conclusions- there is a lot of work remaining in this field. For example, there is no recorded dietary restriction experiment that I could find on human beings. But such experiments on animals began decades ago, and have brought forward surprising results! So why has not an experiment on human-being been done yet? Because these things take time, and are controlled by many factors other than a willing biologist and volunteers. So, what I want to say is- Biology is still immature as far as life history theory is concerned.

So why have *I* stated so many conclusions in this book? ...Because I used a simpler and informal route to the conclusions. It is true that we do not understand exactly how life is born out of molecules. But do we really need to know 'everything' in order to be confident about 'something'? Do we really need to solve the question of life before solving that of 'celibacy'?

It is here that the concept of thermodynamics of biology becomes relevant. We do not know how life works, but we know the motive of life, and hence can predict what an organism should do, and how it should look, in order to survive certain given conditions. And given a set of environmental conditions changing slowly enough over time, an organism will have ample time to adapt to changes, and we can be sure that the organism *would* look the way it *should* look!

But there is a small problem in this assumption. It is not always that the motive of survival decides the traits that an organism will attain. Sometimes simply the laws of chemistry, or we should say- physics, do that! For example, an organism might have certain scaly skin *just* because certain complex molecule is more stable with some other molecule. So life should have any arbitrary form, depending simply upon a given set of underlying physical laws. Hence, it is not always that the motive of survival gives rise to certain traits in an organism. The mutual stability of two bio molecules can also do the same thing! If this is true, our entire assumption in this book would be wrong, because we would now be unable to say anything about life without studying the complex chemical reactions carefully.

Fortunately, this is not generally true. Laws of natural selection, survival of the fittest and elimination of undesirable traits would ensure that life takes a form that is nearly independent of what quantum mechanics wants it to. The form taken by life should depend more on the environmental variables than the laws of physics. We can understand this by considering the following example- imagine that an artist wants to make a painting of a flower. In doing so, he has many choices as to what medium to use- like oil, acrylic, water color, pastels etc. It is true that looking at the final painting, we can immediately tell whether it was made using water color, pastel, or oil etc. Hence, the 'nature' of the medium determines how the output will look. Very true! But think again, the medium of the color decides only a trivial character about the painting. The rest, the subject of the painting itself, enjoys an existence higher than that of choice of the medium, and is determined simply by the motive and inspiration of the artist! It is true that the painting of the flower, painted in oil, pastel or water color would have different appearances. But in each case, the painting is about the *same* thing. The characters are the same, color of the flower, the background, all is same! The *flower* is the same! These characters exist because of the desire of the artist, and are independent of the choice of a medium of the painting.

In the same way, our physical laws control the output, the structure of an organism, but not substantially. There is a different layer of traits decided by the laws of physics and different decided by evolution. The thermodynamics of Biology assumes that the traits decided by the physical laws can be effectively neglected, as far as the theory of trade-off of energy based on priorities is concerned. There are 3 reasons to believe this:-

1. Life has got ample time to circumvent any obstacle brought forward by the physical law in the way of acquiring some trait. The proof is the classic example of bats and birds. Bats and birds both have wings, which are used for a common purpose. Yet the structural origin of the wings of bats is completely different than that of birds. This shows that organisms can reach same state through different routes! Hence given a physical obstacle in acquiring a trait, organisms can always find another route to achieve

the trait, given, of course, ample time, which, in our world, we can safely assume they have had.

2. The traits discussed in this book are very fundamental. So much so, that we have been able to generalize the motive of each organism on earth under it. This trait is that of trade-off of energy between different biological priorities. Every organism must have a list of priorities sorted according to their importance, immediate as well as future ones; and the division of available resources should be decided using an efficient algorithm which recognizes the relative importance of each of the priorities. This is a very basic algorithm required to make a successful organism, one of the first things that you will have to decide if you want to design an organism. So, as far as this algorithm of priorities is concerned, I claim that it is so basic that its existence cannot be decided by existence or non existence of a certain physical law. Any life that is unable to set forward its list of priorities and execute efficient tradeoff of energy between them will die. This is one of the first road blocks that all organisms must overcome, given any set of physical laws. So, drawing from the analogy of paintings, no matter what medium you choose, there will always be a flower in it, because you want there to be one!

3. A multi-cellular organism is formed out of a large number of cells, and is very complex. Hence the total number of combination of molecules and hence the possibilities are very high. Hence, there will be multiple routes to the same objective, making the influence of a set of physical law less important.

So, we have seen that although we do not know the exact chemical mechanism of life, we need not, because we can study life as a bulk process, judging its behavior from its motives; making use of the thermodynamics of biology. This book is about that thermodynamics. We do not know the details of life, but we can study it using approximations. And I have given three reasons why these approximations will be close to correct.

Readers should note that although we have seen some experiments that tend to quantify the loss of energy in a male in the form of semen, I do not intend to claim any proofs based on these experiments. There have been many arguments given by the proponents of celibacy which endow high and sometimes metaphysical nutritional values to semen. For example, it is said in Hindu texts that a drop of white blood (semen) is equivalent to 40 drops of the red ones. I have also come across many sources which try to quantify the nutritional value of semen more scientifically, by giving out the names of some complicated nutrients present in it, which is then claimed to be beneficial for the brain. There also exists the silly Taoist theory that prohibits ejaculation at all cost and instead advices injaculation.

But I do not intend to go in these lines of argument. There are many reasons for this. The most important reason is that some of the above theories are indeed wrong, like those of the Taoists. The second reason is the difficulty of any proof in this line. We have arrived at a more elegant proof through another route... that of the approximation.

Please note that instead of trying to quantify the loss of energy through reproduction, I have instead tried to prove that such loss 'must' exist. I have given experiments in this direction, which actually show it. I have also given mathematical reasons for this to be true, showing that such tradeoff based on priorities is a very good algorithm. So we are at an interesting stage over here- we do not exactly know 'how' reproduction is costly, but we do indeed know that it *is*, and *why* it should be. We know the 'why' of it; we leave the 'how' of it to the professionals.

The fact that the life of an organism needs a perfect balance of priorities is a very beautiful idea. Imagine that you are to create a robot. How will you do that? You will have to make many algorithms which will guide the robot and tell it how to react in order to survive longer. I claim that one of the most fundamental of these algorithms would be that to design a dynamic list of priorities. The ability to decide between two very essential needs is very important. Our robot will die unless it has the ability to discriminate between two apparently equally important needs and choose one of them while discarding the other.

We need some thinking here. A naive algorithm would not do. For example, suppose we need to cross a desert and are allowed a bag full of stuff of our choice. Here comes the important game of choosing between priorities. We need to keep the bag light, but not at the cost of some useful stuff. We need to bring food with us, but not at the cost of water. We will need compass, knife, lighter, but nothing at the cost of anything more important and the risk of making the bag too heavy.

Now, consider another example. Suppose vitamin A is a very necessary nutrient and we will die without it if we do not eat it regularly. Still, our body would not store any more of it for future needs than is required by an unknown equation, an algorithm, which tells how much of it is to be kept. This is because although that vitamin is very necessary, it is not the only necessary thing. And hence, it would be naive to assume that a person who is deficient in a certain vitamin will absorb all of it if the vitamin is suddenly made available to him. Instead, tests show that if given the excess of any nutrient, however important, the body excretes the most of it. This is because of the algorithm of priorities. The body cannot risk too much of anything, because there is limited space to keep things and remain mobile at the same time, and there is a huge dynamic list of priorities to choose from, and an amazingly beautiful involuntary algorithm at work choosing what to keep and how much of it to keep and what to do next.

Many people say that they would give anything to be young again. They do not mean it literally. Such statement is a violation of the algorithm of priorities. There exist prices that are too high. People say things like this out of carelessness and thoughtlessness. If they could give anything to be young again, they would not be old at the first place. So, we can say that in some sense, the philosophy of celibacy is an extremist one... an extreme form of choosing between priorities.

It is really amazing that a body should dump longevity in order to meet more immediate needs. But it is also amazing that a body excretes away the excess part of an important nutrient, however essential it may be. If one thinks a little, one will realize that both these statements are the result of the same algorithm- of deciding between priorities. The one is not more amazing than the other.

Mixing milk in water

Until now, I had a very optimistic view on my theory of celibacy. I made furious adamant statements without ever doubting them. Now, in this section, and this section only, I will try. This will disappoint some of my readers who have credulously believed whatever I have said up till now. To them, I request for patience. It is not that I doubt anything. But it is in the spirit of science that we, for once, may accept that we can be wrong, and look at things from another perspective. For this purpose, I add a new section. This section is complete in itself, and has nothing much to do with my beliefs. One can say that this section emerges more out of an obligation to consider the consequences of being wrong.

I am not completely wrong, if at all. But there are few of my claims that can be doubted. Let me clarify.

I do not doubt that our reproductive priorities cause our aging. This is too beautiful a theory to be wrong. It explains everything. It explains why we age. It gives sense to getting old. It exposes the benefits of getting old. It is not just a biologically correct theory. It is mathematically consistent. It is the result of the algorithm of life. We cannot succeed in making an artificial intelligence if we do not teach our robots how to suspend longevity for more immediate benefits. This is worth a lesson to be learnt and taught.

So, what do I suspect about my theory? What do I doubt?

I doubt whether celibacy can stop aging completely or not. Here, notice that completely is a very exact word. Things can be good, even perfect, without being completely good or perfect. So, I doubt the completeness of my theory. I doubt whether an algorithm, suicidal in nature, which has remained in our body for millions of years, can be 'fooled' through celibacy, so suddenly, to completely stop the aging. I wonder whether the suicidal priorities that drag people to the disease of old age can be cured completely or not.

I have no doubt that celibacy can trigger neurogenesis and boost immunity as never before seen. But I doubt that aging can be completely stopped.

What I mean is- can celibacy stop the suicidal mechanism that exists within us? Can celibacy tell the body, within time, to take the extreme path, and channel all the fuel towards itself, instead of seeking shortcut and passing the torch of life to the next generation?

Can celibacy save the mayfly?

I really don't know. I have reasons to believe it must. I also have reasons to believe it cannot.

For example, there are many scientists who have unknowingly lived long spans of natural celibacy while they were engrossed in the exciting world of science and mathematics, making erotic discoveries in jungle of logic. But even then, these people have tended to neglect themselves in the process. They too started neglecting their longevity for the more immediate need of science. For example, Ramanujan was known to neglect nutrition and sleep when he worked. Same was the case with Tesla, who advised others to not to sleep more than 2 hours every day! We can sense a sharp twist of priorities here. Did these people too compromise their longevity for science and mathematics? Is science simply like sex at a higher level? Does the algorithm of priorities always compromises longevity, no matter what we do? Is it necessary to compromise with future health demise in order to boost present efficiency?

This is the main reason why I suspect the completeness of my theory. Maybe our body is by default designed to compromise longevity and commit suicide, no matter what we do. Maybe it is fate that we must ignore the future for the sake of the present...

But, when it seems that my theory is useless, it has simply changed meaning! If not longevity, then science... if not tomorrow then today... My theory may not help you live 200 years, but it can help you live as if. My theory of priorities is a way of living life. It is a philosophical idea, in which the magnitude of our attempts does not decide what we can achieve, but the direction where we apply it does.

According to the Einstein's theory of relativity, everything in the world moves at the same speed, that of light. Things that look stationary have all their speeds inclined towards the time direction. So, when something moves in space, time slows down for it to balance the overall speed.

Hence, nobody is blessed with a special speed. The fact that an athlete can run faster than others means he can change the direction of his space-time motion, deflecting it a little away from the time direction and more towards the spatial ones. So, it seems that what we do is simply the question of priorities. It depends more on the direction than the magnitude of our efforts. For an athlete, the priority is the joy of chasing people, or leaving them behind!

There is a philosophical idea hidden here. Our speeds are same. Our priorities, the way our efforts are inclined decides what we become. The theory of priorities is a very grand one. Do not commit the mistake of underestimating the power of priorities. Because every moment, the energy we have is being directed towards what we do. And although the energy every moment that is being dissipated is small in magnitude, it is the only possible magnitude of energy which we are capable of using or wasting at any moment of time. So the magnitude of the energy that we use every moment might appear trivial, but it is effectively equivalent to infinity.

Celibacy may not save a scientist, but it will enrich his brain. It will prevent his brain from shrinking over years.

It will give to any person, the most important thing that he wants. The thing that he cares for the most...

....

But again, let's play devil's advocate. Maybe aging *can* be stopped completely. Celibacy on its own cannot ensure that our priorities will get directed towards longevity. We need other ingredients to couple celibacy. We need a healthy life-style, full of sports, nutrition, thinking, adventure and meditation. Once we know the real cause of aging, we, being human being by nature, can certainly change the things of the nature...

There has been immense ancient literature, based on intuition and observation, that advice practices like yoga, meditation and sports as means to improve the quality of life. One can always benefit from them.

The concept of celibacy has arisen in every religion with a reason. This appears to be the natural human tendency... maybe a sub-conscious desire to cherish life as a gift, and live it and live it's every moment.

This reminds me of the lead character of the book- The *Monk who sold his Ferrari*, who returns a changed and young man after his mysterious visit from the Himalayan ranges, and reveals the secrets of the art of living that he has learnt there from a group of mystical sages. I think that Brahmacharya needs to be coupled with a healthy lifestyle to stop aging.

A candle in the darkness

Here, I would like to present for the readers an analogy which beautifully summarizes the message that I wanted to present through this book-

"Imagine a machine with a glowing candle attached to it. In order to prevent the candle from running out of wax, the machine also manufactures some 'new' wax from raw materials and constantly supplies them to the height of the candle.

Let us assume that the machine can manufacture wax at a maximum rate of 10 grams per hour. On the other hand, the rate at which wax can be used up/burnt in the candle is a variable which you can change, let's say, by adjusting a slider on the machine which can make the candle flame get as bright or dim as required.

Now, let us add one last layer of complication: there exists a wind threatening to extinguish the flame. Suppose the risk of getting extinguished by the wind is 20% every hour. This means that if we let 100 identical candles burn for an hour, about 20 of them will get extinguished by the wind by the end of the period.

The question now is- what is the optimum strategy that you can use to get maximum light from the candle for a longer period of time? In other words, at what rate should you let the candle burn?

It can be trivially seen that the optimum strategy cannot be a rate in which less than 10 grams of wax gets used up in an hour. This is because if the rate of usage is less than the rate of manufacture, there will be a net gain in wax at the cost of some brightness of the flame. And given any risk factor (let us say, 20% per hour), the candle will eventually get extinguished, leading to an overall loss in productivity.

But interestingly the rate of usage of exactly 10 grams of wax per hour is also not an optimum strategy, because if the rate of usage is equal to the rate of manufacture, the height of the candle will remain constant, leading to a net wastage of wax when it finally gets extinguished! ...And all of this at the cost of compromised brightness.

In other words, we can increase the lifetime productivity of the candle if we cross the danger line and let it gradually lose height, in a suicidal way, in order to scrape out some last bits of profit from the situation! In other words, the rate of usage of wax should be a calculated bit larger than the rate of manufacture.

This is the optimum strategy. For example, knowing that the risk factor is 20% every hour, I can calculate that the average life-span of such a candle will be 5 hours (This is actually a legitimate question in Probability!). So, in our case, I would adjust the usage of wax in the candle such that it would die on its own after 5 hours and some minutes (I have not actually done the calculations, but intuition tells that the answer should be a little more than the average lifespan).

So, now an interesting question arises- Are we also just like the candle? Do we get old just in order to increase our lifetime productivity? Do we lose health through old age in order to reduce the cost or wastage in the form of our dead bodies?

There is actually a biological theory that says exactly the same thing- that organisms alter their behavior and living pattern and priorities in order to increase the overall productivity of their life. This theory is called 'life history theory'.

Now, the message: We are like burning candles. We are suicidal. Each moment, our metabolism is firing more than it should. Hence make this moment count. Do the things that you always wanted to. There is nothing to lose or gain. It is all in the moment.

Disclaimer: the candle model, although beautiful, does not completely describe human beings because it is too simple to do that. For example, I would have liked to add few more variables, like the rate of change of production of wax with the height of the candle, to illustrate that as our health falls, so falls our ability to recover, as is seen in real aging cases. There are lots of more subtleties. This candle model should be taken as a rough simple model only."

Part3: Philosophical consequence of Brahmacharya

If everyone practices Brahmacharya or celibacy, how will our specie advance?

Well, will everyone practice Brahmacharya? I do not expect them to! And there is no need to look down upon anyone just because they are following celibacy or sexuality. If a person practices strict Brahmacharya, they lose the joys of a sexual life and opportunity to pass their genes to the next generation. If a person follows sexuality with full ardor, they end up degrading their bodies through old age, and suffer reduced cognitive ability over years which may affect their ability to decipher the secrets of the cosmos. So, we are all working as a team, by keeping a race of children coming up, and by living a life filled with explorations.

Suppose humanity represents the mixture of black and white dots. Let white represent Brahmacharya, and black reproduction. From distance, humanity should look grey. If it looks completely white or completely black, the results will be disastrous. If humanity is completely white, we will die due to lack of reproduction. If it is completely black, we will die due to lack of ideas. So, humanity must look grey from distance.

On closure examinations, we may find people who are completely black or white, or those who are a shade in between, depending upon the needs of the individual, depending upon whether they feel inclined towards celibacy or towards sexuality.

The purpose of this book is not to taboo sex. The purpose is to reveal truth about sex which is- in order to increase the chances of sexual success, every organism puts *a little more than due* into sexual expression, *independent* of the amount of resources that are available. This causes old age.

There is no need to taboo sex for this. People love reproduction and having children, and the fact of life is that everything comes at price, and many people are willing to pay for this. Having said this, there are ways that even married people can practice celibacy by spending spells of healthy abstinence if a greater cause arises.

On the other hand, one can allot different time of life for different things. For example, ancient Hindu systems very beautifully allocated first 25 years of life for learning and strict Brahmacharya, and the subsequent years for *Grihast*, or family life. I think that not everybody who does not feels a natural inclination for Brahmacharya should practice it, yet one should have a scientific attitude towards its benefits.

Having said this, those who indeed decide to practice Brahmacharya should go ahead, while at the same time being careful as not to make Brahmacharya the sole motive of their life. Neither sex, nor Brahmacharya should be made the sole motive of one's life, as both of these on their own can be dangerous. Find a motive beyond these things, and seek it through them. Life will become joy to live after that, full of intellectual and physical vigor and fun.

I have enough faith in humanity to believe that not everyone will follow Brahmacharya, yet few will! So extinction of humanity is out of question.

Is there anything more exciting than sex?
Well, this is a difficult question. Sex is very exciting, so much that everyone feels gigantic attraction towards it. Some people

claim that there exists an 'itch' in everyone that only sex can satisfy. There are people who see sex as a mode of understanding themselves and their body. There are people who see mating as a spiritual activity. And then, there are people who have given sex a status of art, by exploring sexuality and by combining it with other human feelings like pain, hate, submission etc to experience the combined effect... There appears to be an entire universe structured over lust and sexual dreams!

Sexuality today is not reproduction to human beings. The fact that people use contraceptives during sex proves it. The fact that people involve in oral and anal sex proves this. The fact that they involve in masturbation, porn viewing and homosexuality proves that sex is not merely reproduction for us. Most human beings do not approach sex as reproduction.

Human beings have begun to treat themselves like algorithm-like machines. You press your *sexual parts* and you feel happiness. Analogously in machines, you press a button and you get a desired result... It seems that a simple algorithm, like pressing a button or not pressing it decides who will be happy at a moment, and who will not be.

It is not healthy to entertain such simple methods of attaining happiness. Because if the artificial intelligence rises to power someday like it did in the movie- *The Matrix*, it may use these simple human algorithms against us, by sending us into the bliss of ignorance, and by pressing our G- or T- spots for us, just to make us happy. If the standard of our happiness are so low and straight forward, we might end up happily in a state of oblivion, living life of illusions in a matrix.

Do you think that the porn addicts of today will really attempt to escape a *Matrix* or computer program which will be giving wings to their wildest fantasies in virtual reality?

Now running the analogy backward, what if we really *are* trapped in a matrix? Just imagine, all of us living peacefully in a world while being completely oblivious about its whereabouts… A world which came from where and is going where, we don't know! How can we spend our days and nights pressing the 'buttons' on us that 'make' us happy, when there is a whole universe awaiting exploration?

Our world is based upon systems of life and birth. But life could not possibly be simply a game of being born and giving birth to someone else. And this is what reality of sex is- it is a subconscious desire to give birth. A sexual act brought us in the world. Life cannot possibly be all about pursuing the same thing…

This brings me back to the physicist and professor joke. All physicists want to become professor. In fact, it is dreams come true for any physicist. So the joke is- you study physics from a professor, and then end up wanting to become another professor who would be teaching many others! So, is this the point of all this? Is this it?

The sole purpose of studying physics cannot be to teach more graduates the same thing. The purpose of studying physics lies elsewhere.

The other form of the same joke is that people are born through sexual reproduction and then end up spending their life in mate searching and mating as if this was the real meaning of life.

This is sex. The question is, is there anything more exciting than sex?

Yes. The thing which is more exciting than sex is the purpose behind life, if you believe in purpose. This world cannot be so meaningless. If sex is so exciting, and at the same time is nothing more than mere an act of giving birth, an act of making new life; then I assert that there exists something that is far superior to sex in its ability to give joy. It must exist... Its existence I predict, just from plain facts that sex is the things that keep the torch of life on, and this proves that the *thing* which we are searching in the light of this torch is *more* worthwhile and exciting than the torch itself, or the fuel of sex fueling it. I assert that the sex, which is the battery of this perennial torch, is far inferior to the cause of the existence of the torch. I predict that mere algorithm based joy, the joy that can be inflicted by a machine on a human, is inferior in its construct. Look around, open your eyes, the truth lie elsewhere...

I predict that this world, this repetitive cycle of life and birth is like an electric pump. The parts of the pump, the fan, the magnet, the support- love doing what they do and keep the machine going forever. The thing that keeps the motor running, the electricity, is sex. The fan, the parts of the pump are the people, moving in a circular motion, repeatedly. For most people, the meaning of this machine ends here. There are they- the fan, and there is the electricity- the sex that becomes the cause and motive for them to keep going. But wait, there is more. There is this *thing* we have not yet discussed- the *purpose* of the pump to exist, which although does not directly concern the fan or the electricity, yet exists, independent of the both. Look at the pump; it is actually throwing out a jet of water towards the cosmos. The high-speed, pearl-like, white water droplets breaking the silence of the universe... this jet of water are no less exciting than the electricity that runs the pump. The complete truth about life is beautiful. The purpose of this pump is more important than its own self. To realize the purpose, one will have to raise higher than the material self of the pump, into the abstract world of sciences, and when one leaves one's material self for science and truth, sexuality and its tiny fluctuations are left behind.

Summarizing the logic used in this section:

Statement 1: Sex is exciting.

Statement 2: Sex is nothing more than reproduction, a method of giving life to new people.

Conclusion: There must exist something in life that is more exciting than sex, namely, the purpose of life, the purpose of all this.

Debate: Statement 1 is undisputable. Statement 2 can be argued upon, trying to establish a higher meaning to sex than mere reproduction, but I can use biological science to falsify this assumption. Other than this, it is up to you to believe what you like, of course. I have nothing to argue upon that.

The Conclusion can be arrived from the two of the statements itself. Some people may claim that there is no '*purpose*' of life. Again, they are free to believe what they like. We are intelligent enough to not start a debate on these matters, because we have left *science* in the last part of this book and are currently in a philosophical regime. If there is an argument against the *scientific parts* of this book, then we can discuss that.

On happiness

I am not a philosopher. I am a to-be-physicist. Hence, I will not force upon you some weird metaphysical view on happiness.

I will instead give a definite scientific and quantitative definition of happiness. So, do not be afraid.

Happiness is not a psychological state. It is more material than that. What is it? Watching comedy shows makes us happy- eating good food, walking in a garden, and being with friends, being healthy, staying safe, wearing good clothes, being loved and respected. All this makes us happy.

But do you understand happiness. Maybe yes. Then answer these questions to test your understanding.

Is there a limit to the amount of happiness a person can feel in a day? Is there a limit after which a person cannot be happier?

Does sadness follows happiness hand in hand? If we simply remove unhappiness from somebody's life, will it make him happy?

Can chemicals and drugs make one happy? What will happen if scientists one day find a safe drug which can induce extreme happiness on simple administration or which can increase the libido of a person indefinitely? Given infinite libido, can masturbation or sexual indulgence make one the happiest person on earth?

Will such hypothetical safe drug be good for humanity or dangerous? Will its use become as necessary and debatable as the use of calculator in school? What, after the introduction of such drug, will be the motive of human survival, if not happiness?

Did you answer all of the questions? Did you feel confident about your view? Do you think you were correct?

All of us try to be happy. We *seek* happiness. The last statement was false. We do not want to be happy in life. Happiness in itself is simply a state of human body and it has no physical meaning. The fact that we seek happiness is false. What our body *really* seeks is the *thing* that makes us happy.

Pay attention, this is important. Every chemical system in the world has a nature. Our body's nature is to survive. Proof- we are alive and trying to maintain that. Now, in order to survive, we recognize some states that increase our chances of surviving... the state of being well fed, the state of being physically fit, the state of having a family and a faithful sexual partner. All these increase our chances of survival. For few of the readers wondering how sexual activity increases our chances of survival, I clarify that it does the job indirectly, by preserving our genes in the next generation the same way our parent's genes are preserved in us. This explains the fact that parents sacrifice their life to save their children in difficult situation. In reality they are not saving somebody else. They are saving a younger, faster and healthier version of their own self, which will easily outlive their present body in similar conditions.

So, here is the conclusion. Happiness is not what we seek. It is the state which causes happiness that we seek. So, eating a hypothetical safe happiness pill will not be the solution to world's problems, because eating such pills does not increase our chances of survival. Such pills will eventually cause mental depression, because the patient will feel guilty as he fades to the background of life and creativity while he is busy giving himself chemical stimulations

Also, there is indeed a physical limit to the amount of happiness one can feel in a day in the same way as there is a limit to amount of good things that one can do in a day. But rest assured, there is no limit to what a person can do given some time, so this limit to happiness a person can feel has no practical meaning.

Happiness and sadness have no relation. The happier you are the less sad you will be.

Now getting to an interesting point- Does watching comedy shows or entertaining movies makes us happy. Yes, but movies have got nothing to do with increasing our chances of survival! Yes it has. Watching movies is a method of relaxation, and people usually watch movies after doing some good but tedious work, like the office work or similar. And office work does increase our chances of survival, because it is important for humanity and together, through our collaboration, we humans as specie have and can outlive mountains and are trying. Plus, in exchange of office work a person gets money which is nothing but a simple certificate of having contributed in human survival which can be exchanged in a shop for more basic needs like food and clothing.

But infinite libido, masturbation and porn cannot make us happy because they would not be contributing towards our chances of survival. These things are like entertainment, and they refresh the mind of people who have had a hard day following orders and living in sub consciously irritable constraints of society. But the question is why would a person involve in such a meaningless and hard lifestyle at all, only seeking brainless entertainments in the end of the day that further saps and causes them to submit to society?

Back Matter

About the author

Jatin Shankar is a 20 years old Indian College student interested in Physics and Mathematics. Jatin wrote this book because he is also interested in the meaning of life and philosophy, and questions like *why we exist…*

Another reason for writing this book was because Jatin, as a teenager, came across some books on Celibacy from *Ramakrishna Mission*, an institute of monks and scholars, where his school would take children to participate in many cultural competitions every winter. It was there that Jatin won the books about Brahmacharya as prize in a competition (Jatin is a good artist!).

Although Jatin was impressed by the idea of Brahmacharya, being a scientific minded kid and an atheist (in the sense that he believes that there is not enough 'data' as yet to settle the question about the existence of god), he decided to find some scientific evidence on the Philosophy of Celibacy before believing in it. He found the clues in the form of thousands of Biological scholarly articles. Jatin admits that he was surprised in how clearly Biology pointed towards the concept of Brahmacharya, and decided to write a book to let others know about this.

Made in the USA
San Bernardino, CA
13 October 2017